MORGANE SCHMIDT

Life with HORSES Is Never ORDERLY

CARTOONS
FOR RIDERS WHO ARE
IN ON THE JOKE

T
TRAFALGAR SQUARE
North Pomfret, Vermont

First published in 2021 by
Trafalgar Square Books
North Pomfret, Vermont 05053

Disclaimer of Liability
The author and publisher shall have neither liability nor responsibility to any person or entity with respect to any loss or damage caused or alleged to be caused directly or indirectly by the information contained in this book. While the book is as accurate as the author can make it, there may be errors, omissions, and inaccuracies.

Trafalgar Square Books encourages the use of approved safety helmets in all equestrian sports and activities.

Library of Congress Cataloging-in-Publication Data
Names: Schmidt, Morgane, author.
Title: Life with horses is never orderly : cartoons for riders who are in on the joke / Morgane Schmidt.
Description: North Pomfret, Vermont : Trafalgar Square Books, 2021. | Summary: "Morgane Schmidt knows all about the madness that comes with the equine territory, having owned and competed horses in eventing and dressage for years. A lifelong fan of the classic equestrian cartoons penned by internationally renowned artist Norman Thelwell, she began her own comic series in 2011, sharing deftly funny reflections on life with horses with an avid online fanbase. Ten years later, her witty observations and fabulously rendered characters have been brought together in one immensely entertaining collection"-- Provided by publisher.
Identifiers: LCCN 2021031897 (print) | LCCN 2021031898 (ebook) | ISBN 9781646010455 (paperback) | ISBN 9781646010462 (epub)
Subjects: LCSH: Horsemanship--Humor.
Classification: LCC SF309 .S354 2021 (print) | LCC SF309 (ebook) | DDC 798.202/07--dc23
LC record available at https://lccn.loc.gov/2021031897
LC ebook record available at https://lccn.loc.gov/2021031898

All illustrations by Morgane Schmidt

Book and cover design by RM Didier

Typefaces: Almaq, Avenir Next Condensed

Printed in the United States of America

10 9 8 7 6 5 4 3 2 1

This book is dedicated to all those who somehow never outgrew the "horse phase."

"It's only forever, not long at all."
–David Bowie

CONTENTS

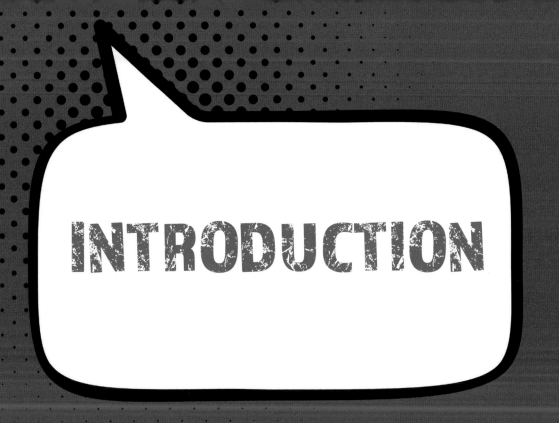

INTRODUCTION

I don't remember an exact moment that I fell in love with horses or when I started to take an interest in visual arts—both just seem to have always been constants throughout my life.

Like so many horse-crazy kids, I collected Breyer® models, wore horribly awkward horse-themed apparel, and made my parents slow down when passing any field that might contain a horse that I could gawk at. In addition to all that, I drew horses obsessively. In fact, early in my childhood I didn't yet have my own horse to usurp all my time, energy, and resources (that was to come when I was fifteen and my pleading finally wore my parents down), so I was able to devote myself to honing my artistic representations of them.

As I got older and my sense of humor a bit wryer (some might even say warped), I also came to appreciate comics and cartooning. Logically, I absolutely adored *Calvin and Hobbes* and Gary Larson's *The Far Side*. When I was finally introduced to Norman Thelwell's iconic ponies, though, it was instant love, as it combined my two favorite things: horses and snark.

A decade or so ago I moved west, and finding myself with some time on my hands, I decided to give creating my own comic a shot. That was the catalyst for *The Idea of Order*. Inspired by Thelwell, with a shot of utter Larson weirdness, and fueled by my entrenchment in equestrian pursuits, *The Idea of Order* is my way of laughing at the inherent absurdities of horse ownership while also embracing the wonderful sense of community that arises when a bunch of masochists can bond over stuff like glittery saddle pads, the bowel movements of an 1,100-pound flight animal, and getting launched into the arena rafters. We really are a special group.

Although some might criticize our somewhat unique life choices and willingness to pour ourselves into caring for an animal who seems intent on killing itself in the most inconvenient, expensive ways possible, I have always found that the equestrian community has afforded me crucial moments of companionship, strength, humor, and inspiration. Horses and art have been a sublime means of communication when I wanted to find a way to reach people and give them a glimpse through my skewed doorway of perception.

What follows is a sort of crash course into the fray that is the horse world. I hope it not only makes you chuckle, but also inspires and reminds you that we should never take ourselves too seriously.

Cheers.

HORSE OWNERSHIP

(Otherwise Known as Character-Building)

Welcome to the most addictive, all-consuming black hole known to man. If you thought the tedious hours spent going through grad school to be an astrophysicist, learning to be an astronaut, running a series of marathons, or spending 47 days hiking in the wilderness were "character-building," you should go ahead and buckle up now because you ain't seen nothin' yet. As adamantly as we love them, you have to admit that horses are a unique sort of chaos that never fails to challenge us physically and mentally. This chapter considers some of the ways horses make us better people in spite of ourselves.

Horses:
The Ultimate in Character Building

The things horses teach us....
This could possibly explain why
there are so many "unique characters"
(aka wackadoos) in the horse world.
I don't know about the rest of you, but I
certainly know that I've embarked on many
character-building activities with each
of my horses—some of which even
taught me useful things (like
to always be aware of
my surroundings).

Equine Risk Assessment:
An Owner's Guide

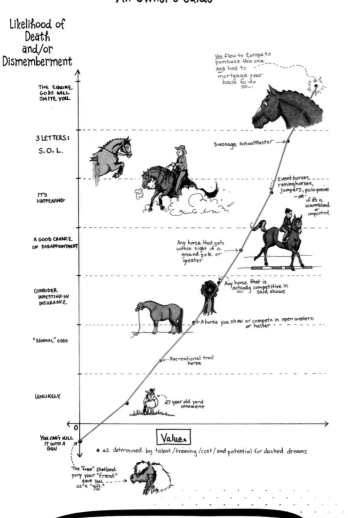

Likelihood of Death and/or Dismemberment

- THE EQUINE GODS WILL SMITE YOU
- 3 LETTERS: S.O.L.
- IT'S HAPPENING
- A GOOD CHANCE OF DISAPPOINTMENT
- CONSIDER INVESTING IN INSURANCE.
- "NORMAL" ODDS
- UNLIKELY
- 0
- YOU CAN'T KILL IT WITH A GUN

Value*

* as determined by talent / training / cost / and potential for dashed dreams

Labels on chart:
- You flew to Europe to purchase this one. AND had to mortgage your house to do so...
- Dressage schoolmaster
- Event horses, reining horses, jumpers, polo ponies — or — if it's a warmblood or imported
- Any horse that gets within sight of a ground pole or greater
- Any horse that is actually competitive in said shows
- A horse you show or compete in open western or halter
- Recreational trail horse
- 27 year old yard ornament
- The "free" Shetland pony your "friend" gave you as a "gift."

Horses are a risky investment at best and a terrible financial crisis at worst. For all of you in search of an easy way to determine how likely your horse is to kill himself in his lush pasture and padded stall, I've created this handy little chart. You're welcome.

Every. Single. Time.
It never seems to fail: Just when you think you've got your horse figured out he has to go and prove you wrong (in all the worst ways, usually). I'm fairly convinced horses do this for their own personal amusement; I mean, what else do they have to do?

CHALLENGE ACCEPTED...

"Oh, he should be fine. He's never done anything stupid like that before."

"Hold my beer."

Horse: *noun*

1) A four-legged mammal looking for an inconvenient place and an expensive way to die. Any day they choose not to execute the Master Plan is just one more to perfect it.

No one needed a dictionary to figure this one out. (Okay, so maybe this isn't *exactly* how Merriam-Webster defines it, but it *is* more accurate.)

Worries.
They certainly vary by species.
I tend to be a worrier by nature, and when it comes to my horses, I'm actually a little crazy (admit it, you all are too). Of course, even though I spend 98 percent of my day concerned that my herd has done something expensive, stupid, or vet-worthy, I am sure they remain unburdened by such silliness.
Good for them, I suppose.

Things I have Worried About Today, as a Horse Owner:

- Did he take a funny step behind yesterday or am I imagining it?
- Maybe my footing is too deep.
- I hope that new hay is high enough quality but also low in sugar.
- He was awfully close to the fence line this morning. I wonder if the hot wire is grounding out somewhere?
- Is he getting along with his neighbor or have they dismantled the fence?
- He better not have his leg caught in the fence!
- Shoot, did I leave the muck fork within reach outside his pen?
- RIP Muck fork.
- Is his fly sheet going to be too warm today?
- Maybe he needs a fan?
- Crap, what if the fan starts a fire?
- Is he going to go nuts when the garbage truck goes by?
- I wonder if I need to pick up more grain?
- I hope his supplements came today; he'll transform into a fire breathing dragon if he misses a day.
- Did I turn off the hose?
- Did I latch both gates and snap them?
- Oh, God, I don't remember doing the latches! He's probably loose & running amok down the road!

Things my Horse has Worried About Today:

I wonder when the Small Predator will be back to give me more sustenance and shower me with much deserved adoration?

Finding the 'Perfect' Breeches:

A quest on par with the search for the holy grail.

High Waisted Breeches

These make you look like you just stepped out of the days of yore. they are a super choice though if 'the ladies' would like a little 'extra support.'

Light Weight Breeches

An excellent selection for those wishing to share every panty-line, bump, bulge, and imperfection with the world. For everyone else these are probably a poor choice.

Low Rise Breeches

These work best for those pranksters who enjoy mooning people and those who delight in indulging an OCD-like compulsion to pull up their pants.

Unfortunate Seam Placement Breeches

These are for the purely masochistic and should probably be avoided by the general populace.

Like finding a unicorn....
Actually, a unicorn is easier and less painful to find.
For those of us not gifted with bodies like Greek gods, breeches–like bikinis and form-fitting evening wear–are just one of those things that take a lot of work to get right. Ideally you can find a pair that are both comfortable and flattering. Sometimes, though, I've been known to settle for simply comfortable and not entirely grotesque. Life's a compromise.

"Seriously? WHY? Is this how you show your gratitude for all I do to take care of you?"

"Nope. It's just because I can."

Poo soup... one more way to ruin your day. Because why shouldn't horses poop in little bowls of water too? Oh, yeah, because then *we* get to clean them. Ugh.

Who knew steel shoes don't float? My horses are masters of losing things they don't like. Unfortunately, I'm less of a master at finding said things until they have begun to properly decay.

"I'll give you a hint: you'd have better luck finding the Lost City of Atlantis or the Loch Ness Monster."

Equine Scavenger Hunt:

A merry chase, indeed.
It would seem negotiations have
gone south. A great cardiac routine
for both horse and rider.

Who doesn't like to play "Hide and Seek"? I mean, really, what else do you have to do with your time? Especially when it degenerates into "Spin and Bolt" around the Back Forty. It's a good thing that both my beasts are so food-motivated I could lay a trail of sugar cubes from the gate to the cross-ties and they'd follow it...right on up to the point when they'd spy the halter and "Spin and Bolt" would commence.

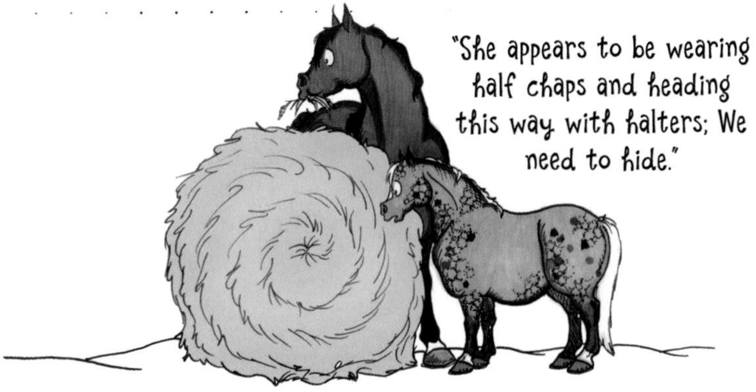
"She appears to be wearing half chaps and heading this way with halters; We need to hide."

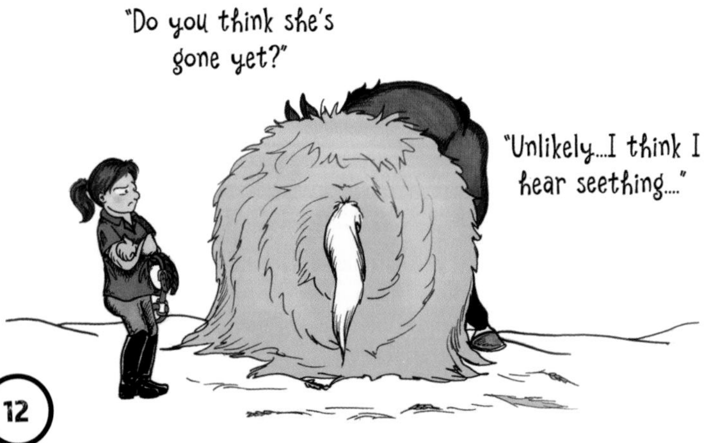
"Do you think she's gone yet?"
"Unlikely...I think I hear seething...."

Books I could write as an equestrian:

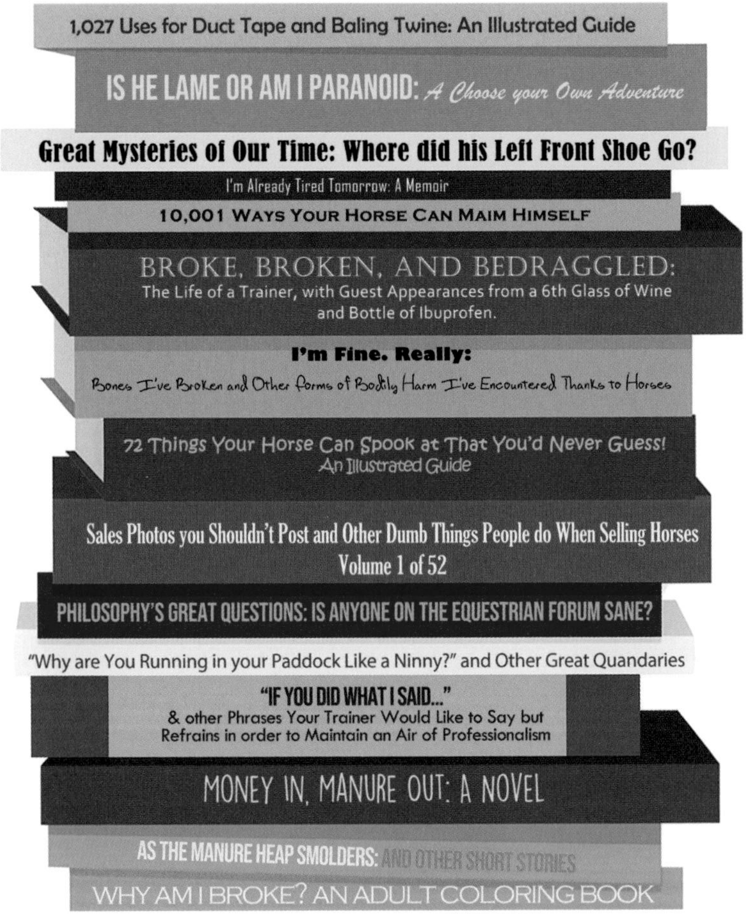
1,027 Uses for Duct Tape and Baling Twine: An Illustrated Guide
IS HE LAME OR AM I PARANOID: A Choose your Own Adventure
Great Mysteries of Our Time: Where did his Left Front Shoe Go?
I'm Already Tired Tomorrow: A Memoir
10,001 WAYS YOUR HORSE CAN MAIM HIMSELF
BROKE, BROKEN, AND BEDRAGGLED:
The Life of a Trainer, with Guest Appearances from a 6th Glass of Wine and Bottle of Ibuprofen.
I'm Fine. Really:
Bones I've Broken and Other forms of Bodily Harm I've Encountered Thanks to Horses
72 Things Your Horse Can Spook at That You'd Never Guess!
An Illustrated Guide
Sales Photos you Shouldn't Post and Other Dumb Things People do When Selling Horses
Volume 1 of 52
PHILOSOPHY'S GREAT QUESTIONS: IS ANYONE ON THE EQUESTRIAN FORUM SANE?
"Why are You Running in your Paddock Like a Ninny?" and Other Great Quandaries
"IF YOU DID WHAT I SAID..."
& other Phrases Your Trainer Would Like to Say but Refrains in order to Maintain an Air of Professionalism
MONEY IN, MANURE OUT: A NOVEL
AS THE MANURE HEAP SMOLDERS: AND OTHER SHORT STORIES
WHY AM I BROKE? AN ADULT COLORING BOOK

Books I should consider writing.... Seriously, these would be bestsellers. Of course, I am fairly certain most equestrians could pen similar titles.

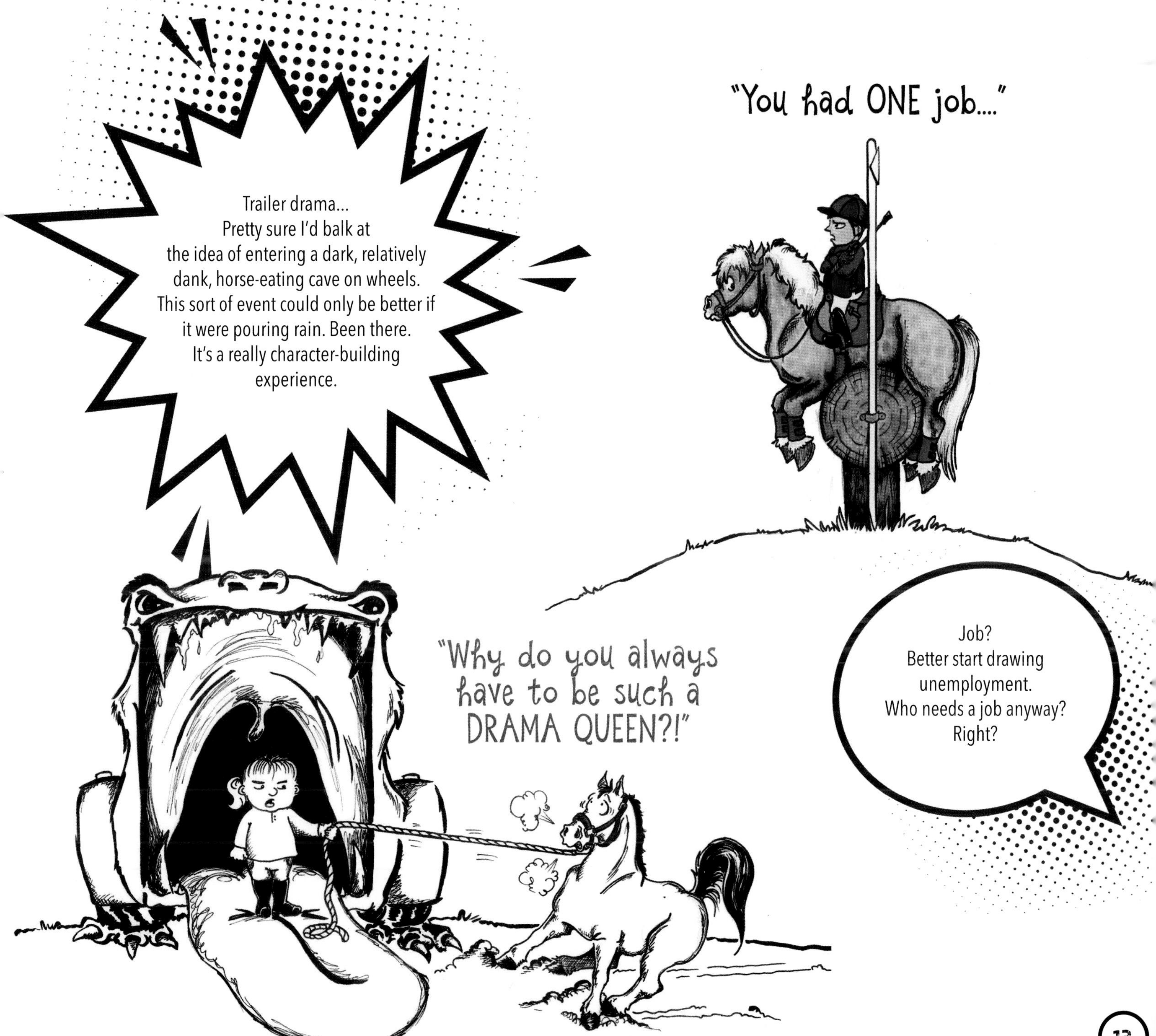
Trailer drama... Pretty sure I'd balk at the idea of entering a dark, relatively dank, horse-eating cave on wheels. This sort of event could only be better if it were pouring rain. Been there. It's a really character-building experience.
"You had ONE job...."
"Why do you always have to be such a DRAMA QUEEN?!"
Job? Better start drawing unemployment. Who needs a job anyway? Right?

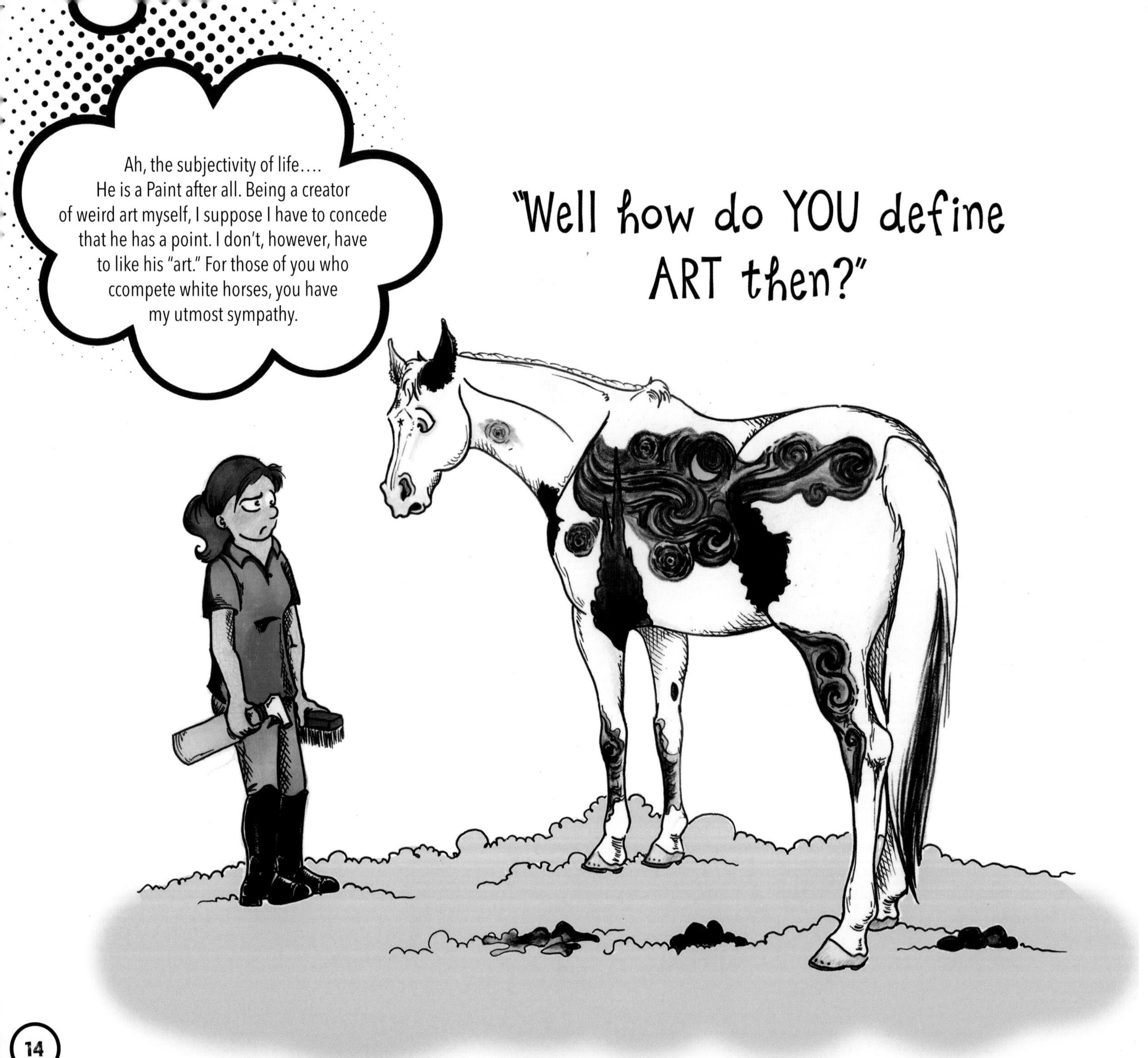
Ah, the subjectivity of life.... He is a Paint after all. Being a creator of weird art myself, I suppose I have to concede that he has a point. I don't, however, have to like his "art." For those of you who ccompete white horses, you have my utmost sympathy.
"Well how do YOU define ART then?"

Horse Forums...
An Inevitable Train Wreck

Susie Q. [Posts: 4]
Hi everyone! My Arab gelding has been acting buddy sour when I take him away from his pasture mate. Do you think it would help to separate them?

DressageLurver [Posts: 5,921]
I can't believe you have TWO horses turned out TOGETHER! Don't you know they could lame each other? I HIGHLY suggest you get them both their own 12x12 stall ASAP!

Nat-Chew-Rowel [Posts: 107]
You can't separate them! It's unhealthy. They need the physical contact of their herd members. You should play 7 Games with your gelding until you two reach a new level of oneness and understanding, then he will follow you willingly wherever you want to go and be your best friend.

MunByProx [Posts: 619]
Have you had the vet out? He's probably lame. You need to rule out lameness before you do anything else. He may be nappy to leave his friend because he's sore.

HoofBeatz [Posts: 89]
Why would you even own an Arab?! They're crazy! Get rid of them both!

QtPie [Posts: 1]
RIDING HORSIESSS ISSS MEEAANNN!

Kollector [Posts: 459]
My neighbor once separated her two horses. One then ran through a fence to get to the other and shredded his legs up. It was pretty terrible. I'd get a third horse to keep one company.

R.A.R.A! [Posts: 5]
I agree with QtPie! You shouldn't even RIDE horses! You're basically enslaving sentient beings to do your bidding. It's just wrong!

AlterHalter65 [Posts: 15]
The OP is a TROLL and just trying to stir up stuff because she has a beef with the barn manager!

GitErDone1455 [Posts: 329]
Of course you should separate them!! That's the only way they will learn.

RailBird [Posts: 21,876]
I can't believe the awful advice you're getting! Everyone here is a total idiot. I sent you a PM.

OldNag [Posts: 25,078] Ignore RailBird, she's always got her panties in a knot. I'm not sure why they still let her post here!

PreVet [Posts: 324]
It's ulcers. It's always ulcers.

Page 1 of 78 Next

Because we all know advice from the Interwebz is always super solid…and super snarky. Who doesn't enjoy reading a good train wreck from the comfort of their own home (preferably with some wine or a latte)? Of course, as much as I may poke fun at said forums, I have gotten some pretty decent advice on a few of them (you just have to be able to filter through the more "speshul" responses).

"What are you doing?"

"Confirming my suspicion that horse people are all crazy."

"Ah. Indeed."

15

> Horses (at least mine) seem to have myriad ways to test our patience and spend our money. Of course, sometimes it really is a toss-up if it's worse to be on the sending or receiving end of these sorts of calls.

Phone Calls:

Some are more painful than others.

What Your Vet Says:

"So it appears that the vessel is thickened and active but I don't see any holes or obvious tears to the superficial flexor tendon, the deep digital flexor tendon, or the suspensory ligament.
Let's give him some time off and recheck in ten days."

What You Hear:

"Blah, blah, blah, THICKENED AND ACTIVE, blah, blah, TEARS, blah, blah, SUPERFICIAL FLEXOR TENDON, DEEP DIGITAL FLEXOR TENDON, SUSPENSORY LIGAMENT, blah, blah, TIME OFF..."

> Usually I consider myself fairly intelligent. I can generally follow a conversation and read for comprehension; sometimes I even add insightful comments. Unfortunately, all that goes out the window when my horse has maimed himself and the vet is involved. At that point, usually when the vet is explaining what's up, my brain takes a momentary hiatus and all I hear is the potential doom. It's a super-fun skill.

On a schedule? Bahahaha! Good luck with that. It never fails. Horses are always a huge time suck, but they turn into a time black hole if you're even remotely in a hurry. Good thing I've conditioned everyone to my perpetual tardiness.

When you ONLY have an Hour to Ride:

"Really? Was this necessary?"

Famous Last Words:

"This horse is BOMBPROOF! Beginners ride this horse. My GRANDMA rides this horse!"

Define "ride." And is your grandma a professional bronc rider? My dad always said never to brag on a horse because the horse would always let you down. While that seems to be perhaps overly pessimistic, I can't help but think there's a grain of truth to it. Not because horses want to let us down, but because Murphy's law is a force to be reckoned with.

How to Read Horse Sale Ads:

"He's 16+ hands tall."
READ AS: He's probably 15.2, MAYBE 15.3 on a good day while being measured on a hill...

"He's a good eater."
READ AS: I've got nothing better to say about this horse.

"Requires a tactful rider."
READ AS: Must have the hands of a bomb squad technician and the balls of Chuck Norris.

"Is sensitive to his surroundings."
READ AS: He spooks at everything from butterflies, to invisible trolls, to rogue nations."

"Horse is very animated/spirited."
READ AS: He sees dead people and will frequently give you the opportunity to join them."

"Needs experienced rider."
READ AS: Horse NOT for the faint of heart (or those without hearty health insurance)."

"Homebred."
READ AS: This horse may very well kill you due to lack of manners."

"Beautiful Warmblood cross." (No lineage listed)
READ AS: Horse is of questionable origins but is too big and slow to be a TB.
-OR-
We just really want to jack the price up another 10k by claiming he's a warmblood of some sort.

"Her 1/2 sister is a National Champion."
READ AS: She's obviously not her sister (which is why we are selling her), but you can always dream and hope the parent they shared was the one responsible for the talented genes.

"Eligible for registration..."
READ AS: With a questionable registry *if* you can track down the papers documenting her lineage for the past five generations on both sides and pay a hefty fee.

Who hasn't had the "fun" of horse shopping and being shown horses that weren't quite what they'd seemed in their ads? It's almost as much fun as going on a blind date with someone billed as 6'2" with a wicked sense of humor and instead meeting a 5'7" wallflower who thinks horses are frightening (true story…). In any event, in an effort to avoid those sorts of scenarios, I've compiled this handy little list to help you better translate what those ads are really saying.

"Always in the ribbons."
READ AS: They were mostly pink and green in shows with no more than 5 or 6 per class which is why we didn't specify her placings.

"Aged gelding."
READ AS: See image below.

"Broke to death."
READ AS: See image below.

"Needs some maintenance."
READ AS: See image below.

"Free horse."
READ AS: This is a farce; you might as well start dropping your money in now. If you're smart you will RUN AWAY AND NEVER LOOK BACK.

Horse Order Form:

Find your next Soulmate!

Breed*:_____ Sex:____ Age:____ Height:____

*ADD **10%** TO BASE PRICE FOR WARMBLOOD BREEDS

Color:
- ☐ Chestnut
- ☐ Bay
- ☐ Grey
- ☐ Black*
- ☐ Palomino*
- ☐ Buckskin*
- ☐ Paint
- ☐ Appy
- ☐ Roan
- ☐ Cremello
- ☐ Perlino
- ☐ OTHER (*please specify*):_____

*ADD **5%** TO BASE PRICE

Color Add-ons:
- ☐ Full Chrome Package*
- ☐ Socks
- ☐ Blaze
- ☐ Star
- ☐ Stripe
- ☐ Snip
- ☐ Other (*Please specify*):_____

*ADD **5%** TO BASE PRICE

Soundness:
- ☐ Mostly Lame
- ☐ Slightly Lame-ish
- ☐ Moderately Sound
- ☐ Totally Sound*

*ADD **10%** TO BASE PRICE

Level of Training:
- ☐ Feral
- ☐ Reasonable Prospect
- ☐ Started
- ☐ Someone Sat on it and Didn't Die
- ☐ Moderately Trained
- ☐ Champion of the World
- ☐ Any Idiot can Make this Animal Perform*

*ADD **10%-15%** TO BASE PRICE

Mental Soundness:
- ☐ Dead
- ☐ More 'Whoa' than 'Go'
- ☐ Moderate Go
- ☐ Sensitive but Sane*
- ☐ Rear on Fire
- ☐ You have something to prove...

*ADD **10%** TO BASE PRICE

Show Record (?):
- ☐ Yes*   ☐ No

*ADD **10%** TO BASE PRICE

Personality:
☐ Apathetic to Your Existence
☐ Stoic
☐ Friendly
☐ Actually Likes You
☐ In Your Pocket
☐ Borderline Pushy
☐ Aggressive
☐ Everyone but You Hates this Horse

Vices (?):
☐ None OK*
☐ Cribber
☐ Weaver
☐ Screamer
☐ Bucker
☐ Rearer
☐ Bolter
☐ Biter
☐ Fence Breaker
☐ Stall Destroyer
☐ Blanket Shredder
☐ General PITA
☐ Other (*please specify*):_____
*ADD 10%-15% TO BASE PRICE

Other Notes:_____
_____
_____
_____

Color Add-ons:
☐ Full Chrome Package*
☐ Socks
☐ Blaze
☐ Star
☐ Stripe
☐ Snip
☐ Other (*Please specify*):_____
*ADD 5% TO BASE PRICE

'Personalized' Receipt:
☐ None
☐ Husband/Significant Other
(PRICE LISTED AT 10% LOWER THAN ACTUAL)
☐ Bragging Rights
(PRICE LISTED AT 10% HIGHER THAN ACTUAL)

'Unicorn' Option (?):
A BEAST OF NEARLY MYTHICAL AWESOMENESS
THAT ONLY ONE CAN EXIST ON THE PLANET AT
ANY GIVEN TIME.
☐ Yes*   ☐ No
**MAY DELAY SHIPPING. CURRENTLY
BACKORDERED UNTIL 2025.*

If horse shopping was easy…or sane. Another word would be sane. Really, what more is there to say? If you've ever been horse shopping you know how absurdly time-consuming, gut-wrenching, and soul-sucking it can be.

Delivery and final purchase price of horse will be confirmed after this order form is received. Returns are accepted for a nominal re-stocking fee. Horse warranty included for 1 year after purchase date.

As if taking on a mature, trained horse doesn't offer enough excitement and anxiety. Many a savvy horseman has acquired a real gem by buying what looked like a mutant camel as a two-year-old. Of course, others have simply acquired a mutant camel.

Two Year Olds:
Because why should the front legs and hind end match?

"I'm just going to turn you out for another six months, perhaps BEHIND the barn, and hope this is just a phase...."

Unfortunate Equine Truth #18:

If you want to be a FABULOUS rider, you can't just do this:

You must also suffer THIS:

Simple fact:
I didn't want to believe this but, alas, it's true. Particularly if you have an athletic equine partner to keep you on your toes (or bouncing gracefully out of the tack). This is almost as depressing as the fact that I can't live on white bread and sugar without turning into the Stay-Puft Marshmallow Man.

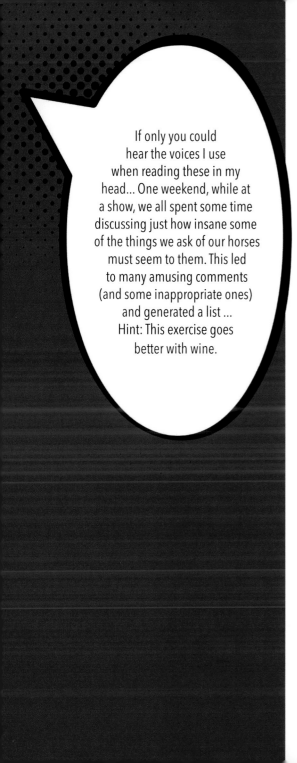

Equine Vocabulary Words:
As Defined By Horses Themselves

Small Predators (AKA Staff): Those are the two-legs that wander about. Some are more friendly than others. They usually provide you with room service, treats, and cleaning. They also occasionally leap on your back but unlike most predators these don't usually try to eat you (though some are more bitey than others...).

Small Predator Claws: These are good for getting scritchies if you can convince your predator to do it. They're also good for solving latch games and opening grain containers and stall doors.

Bossy Pointy Predator: She often crouches in the bushes by the ring and all you can see are her pointy black ears. This predator is much more annoying than the small predators because she runs around barking orders. If you make a snarlyface at her and stomp sometimes she will leave but she usually comes back. Sometimes the small predators tie her up which is funny.

Predator Grain: The stuff predators eat that's usually better than what you have. If you beg and look pathetic enough sometimes they share. If you're fast enough, sometimes you can steal.

Teleporting Bear Cave: This is a big metal bear cave that usually doesn't have a bear in it but isn't much fun nonetheless (sometimes if you refuse to get in it it DOES have an angry small predator in it...). You get in this and after an indeterminate amount of time and much bouncing around you appear somewhere else, usually accompanied by your predator who somehow wasn't in the cave with you.

Firstshow: This is apparently a thing. Your predator will take you somewhere in the teleporting bear cave and there will be MANY sights, sounds, other horses, and spookyf*@#ingb*llsh*t that you're not allowed to look at. You'll also have to have your hair pulled tight on top of your head and spend a lot of time waiting around. I'm not sure entirely what the point is but it seems important to the predators. I recommend being very friendly and talking to all the other horses far and wide. See if you can get the entire show in on the conversation; it's good networking.

Small Pond: These are usually found in your stall or paddock. They're good for drinking but even more fun for sinking inconvenient items in (flyhats, brushes, empty grain pans...). If the small predators are being especially stinky you can poop in them.

Flyhat: A stupid net the small predators make you wear on your head over your eyes. I think the point is to see who can get theirs off first. Help your friends with this. These are good for sinking in the small pond.

Bite-Face: A game to play with your friends where you bite their faces; whoever is bleeding less at the end wins. This is usually played over the fence until the small predators notice and string up biting wire between you. Sometimes one of you can take one for the team and pull down the wire to continue playing.

When You Have Horses at Home...

Who Needs the Gym?

Gym? Pshhh....That's for people who board their horses. I admittedly do still go to the gym because, you know, it's kind of required when you enjoy eating like I do. But I do get quite a bit of daily activity in just making sure the herd gets taken care of.

Oh, so you wanted to show? That's cute.

Never. Fails.

"What happened?"

"I entered him in a show this weekend."

If Equestrians were Honest with Their Facebook Posts:

★ Had a totally mediocre ride today at the show and fell middle of the pack in the class. #Standard

★ I haven't washed my saddle pad since I bought it...a year ago. Still not going to. #Durable

★ I didn't clean my bridle today. Probably won't tomorrow either. #BitGritTreats

★ Won my class today because I was the only one in it. #RockStar

★ Used the same bridle on two horses because I didn't want to clean two.

★ Rode bareback today because I'm too lazy to tack up.

★ Body clipped my horse this afternoon and saved the legs for later. #NeverGonnaHappen

★ Didn't have clean, matching polo wraps for the dressage clinic...rode in open front jumping boots. #ThatsHowIRoll

★ Went to the barn with the intent to ride my horse but instead talked to four people, ran out of time, and gave him a carrot. #GoingPlaces

★ I don't remember the last time I brushed my horse's tail. #GroomingForTheWin

★ I jumped cross rails today. #Tokyo2020

★ Today I worked on transitions. We walked a lot. #NextIsabellWerth

★ I did horse laundry in our house washer without removing the hair first. #TheItchingIsInYourHeadDear

★ Horse people are crazy. I am not an exception. #Honesty

★ Someone was hogging the bathroom, so I peed in my horse's stall while chatting with the people in the barn aisle. #Modesty #SorryNotSorry

If Facebook posts were true...there'd be ones even worse than these, I'm sure. Everyone posts their highlight reel. While that's understandable, it can make the outtake reel that you're living (i.e. your real life) feel somehow less than awesome.

Mystery Lamenesses...

"Well, he's lame somewhere on the left front–and maybe left hind–but it mostly blocked out somewhere below the knee on the front. Or, we think it did. But there isn't anything on the 47 x-rays or the ultrasound. It could be a collateral ligament, a bone bruise, or cartilage lesion but those only show up on an MRI. I guess it could also be neck arthritis, Lyme, EPM, kissing spine, bad karma, demons, or another leg."

"So what did the vet say?"

"Uh, wow. So what are you doing for it?"

"Probably a jug of cheap wine and a bottle of antidepressants."

"Oh...will those help him?"

"No. But I'll feel better."

Doing their Part to Help the Economy!
Particularly the Alcohol and Pharmaceutical Industries

Helping the economy…
that's what I tell myself, anyway.
Anyone ever been here? While slowly driving themselves utterly batshit.

GOOD BARN-KEEPING

(The Life of a Serf)

Even when things are going relatively to plan, horses are entropy, an entropy that equestrians must learn to juggle with something akin to finesse (denial, alcohol, coffee, and narcotics are your friends). More specifically, horse ownership doesn't simply mean manual labor and myriad chores, it also involves spending an inordinate amount of time trying to keep your horse alive, sound, and generally "happy" (because horses get ulcers faster than you can say, "Pass the merlot"). In any event, this chapter explores some of those challenges and even some of the ways we harass them back. I do not, however, make any promises that it offers you viable solutions.

Staff....
Some of us have it, some of us ARE it.
Oh, but we are there for *their* entertainment. One hundred percent, in fact. I'm also fairly certain that my horse is convinced that he has an extensive staff that's been hand-selected to attend to his every need. The sad thing is he's not really wrong about that.

"Hello, Favorite Human!
I see that you're doing things. I'll just stand here and wait...and breathe on you....
Do you perchance have a cookie?
I think I smell a cookie..."

"You know, I am not here for your entertainment."

"You're funny.
Will any of my other staff be in today?"

Horses "Helping:"
It's all fun and games...

Until it's NOT.

Such generous creatures....
and so good at keeping the small predators "entertained." Mine always decide to help when I'm pressed for time;
they're so thoughtful.

How does your horse enjoy the weekend? Mine especially enjoy this over New Year's and Christmas. Doesn't it always seem to be just at the most inopportune moment that your horse maims himself or suddenly has the worst colic in history? Yeah, mine too.

The Top 5 Most Annoying Moments when Cleaning Stalls:

5. The moment you realize that you will indeed need to move that MASSIVE pile of pony poo that you've managed to balance precariously in ONE wheelbarrow load (my aren't we the victim of our own poor choices).

4. The moment you realize you'll need to strip the stall for the 3rd time this week because your horse likes to see how much pee he can produce in a 24-hour period.

3. The moment you realize that your horse has pooped in his BAZILLION gallon water bucket IN his stall - which is actually a trash can and has no drain, so you'll be bailing that sucker out- turning it into some sort of poo slurry.

2. The moment you realize that all your hard work mucking your horse's stall... Is really just an exercise in futility.

1. The number one, most annoying, swear-worthy moment while cleaning stalls is when you throw off your entire groove by slamming the pitchfork into the stall wall, door, or a wayward stall mat that subsequently flings poo everywhere, destroying whatever progress you may have made.

Don't lie, we've all been here. As if scooping WHEELBARROW-LOADS of excrement isn't annoying enough in and of itself, there are still those special moments that really make you want to scream (or, if you're like me, swear violently, likely scaring the poor horse simultaneously).

Because horses never stop testing us. I can't be the only one who cringes slightly when I let my beast loose. I know he *needs* the time to move around, but I'm not always sure I trust him to keep himself alive for more than an hour or two tops.

Turning my Horse Out:

"Make GOOD choices..."

The Myth of Sisyphus:
Equestrian Edition

Sisyphus MUST have been an equestrian....
It. Just. Never. Ends.
If you're not up on your mythology, this may not be such a great comic, but I feel like any horse person can still understand the futility here.

Speaking of turnout, here's a stroke of genius: You know you've at least considered this option... If only my horse thought this was as swell an idea as I do. Perhaps a giant hamster ball would suit him better.

Warmblood Turnout Wrap
Also GREAT for Shipping!

If Your Horse had a Planner:

MONDAY
7:30 Wait for Catered Breakfast
8:00 Maid Service
9:00 Body Work
10:30 "Guided Exercise" with the Small Predator
12:00 Noonsies
5:00 Catered Dinner
9:00 Night Snack

TUESDAY
7:30 Catered Breakfast
8:00 Maid Service - Stand in the Middle and Watch
9:00 Acupuncture Session 1
10:30 Turnout Time
12:00 Noonsies
5:00 Catered Dinner
9:00 Night Snack

WEDNESDAY
7:30 Catered Breakfast
8:00 Maid Service
10:30 Beg Treats off the Small Predators in the Barn
12:00 Noonsies
1:00 Pedicure with the farrier
5:00 Catered Dinner
9:00 Night Snack

THURSDAY
7:30 Catered Breakfast with Maid Service
8:00 Entertain the Small Predator in the Big Sandbox
10:30 Acupuncture Session 2
12:00 Noonsies and Naps
2:00 Body Clip and Spa Day
5:00 Catered Dinner and Break in new Blanket/Chew Toy
9:00 Night Snack

FRIDAY
7:30 Catered Breakfast with Maid Service
8:30 Watch Small Predator Collect Scraps of New Chew Toy
11:00 Chiropractor
12:00 Noonsies
2:00 Massage
5:00 Catered Dinner with Old Blanket Again
9:00 Night Snack

SATURDAY
7:30 Throw a Glorious Bucking Fit at Late Breakfast
8:00 Breakfast and Maid Service
10:00 Humor Trainer Lady that She's Worth Listening to
12:00 Noonsies
1:00 Nap in the Sun
5:00 Catered Dinner
9:00 Night Snack

SUNDAY
7:30 Pace Fence Line in an Agitated Manner and Scream for Breakfast
8:00 Breakfast and Maid Service - Pee in New Shavings
11:00 Self-guided Field Trip Across the Property (Small Predator may Hang on or Not)
12:00 Noonsies
5:00 Catered Dinner
9:00 Night Snack

GOALS

Optimize all eating and napping times.

Humor small predator, but minimize work.

TO DO

1. Eat ALL the things.
2. Poop.
(Small predators worry when you don't.)
3. Nap.
4. Charm small predators for glorious pocket findings.
5. More pooping!

NOTES

-Wait until the farrier leaves before pulling shoes back off.
-Look innocent.
-Don't bite the vet even if she deserves it.

His planner versus yours…. Because we know all their shenanigans are basically premeditated. There's so much here that I'm not even sure what to aim my snarkiness at— the coddled nature of our beasts? The time and money sink that they inevitably are? The fact that most equestrians would likely bleed out before seeing a doctor, but if Dobbin has a hang nail they call the vet, the farrier, and a priest to fix it? We're certainly a… dedicated bunch.

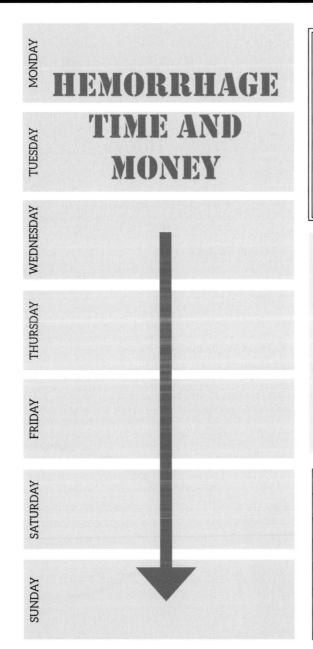

MONDAY	**HEMORRHAGE TIME AND MONEY**
TUESDAY	
WEDNESDAY	
THURSDAY	
FRIDAY	
SATURDAY	
SUNDAY	

GOALS

Keep that JERK sound and alive!

TO DO

- Schedule vet, farrier, body worker, saddle fitter, and chiropractor.
- Order hay and grain.
- Barn chores X 100.
- Make sure Dobbin doesn't kill himself.
- Work to pay for His Highness.

NOTES

I should probably go to the actual grocery store and do some human laundry this week...

Top Ten Ways to Bring About Lameness
(in the not so distant future)

10. Actually like the horse you currently own.

9. Have the audacity to want to ride & show said horse you like & own.

8. Purchase new show gear; even when you never get to use it you're still stimulating the economy.

7. Casually think to yourself that it's been awhile since you've chatted with the vet.

6. Step up & get a USDF lifetime registration for your horse.

5. Redo all your pasture fencing; your horses will find any nails you missed & bring them to your attention.

4. Drop your horse's major medical coverage (this usually ensures he will just experience a career ending injury but will remain otherwise entirely healthy...).

3. Buy a quality youngster; those are always good for gaining hands on veterinary experience.

2. Send in your entry—& proper health certificates & coggins paperwork— to the non-refundable rated show that's two states away; don't forget to book your hotel room too.

1. Utter the phrase "He's never taken a lame step."

you might as well poke the Equine God in the eye with a sharp stick

I speak from a place of experience on this...or you can also just be me. That's also a super way to ensure your horse will go lame. This is the story of my life.

It never fails to cost me tons of time and money. Given how often this happens, I'm fairly certain my horses fail to appreciate how much time and money I invest in their safety and comfort. If they did appreciate it, they surely wouldn't destroy every article of apparel I get them or hide it among the puddles and shrubbery in the pasture. Or at least…I would hope not.

It Never Fails:

When I turn my horse out…

When I go to bring him in…

While I'm Looking…

When I Turn Around…

Sibling rivalry. Despite me telling Woody it would be in his best interests not to antagonize the large, black beast that lives beside him, he just can't seem to help himself. After watching Flirt pick him up by the rump of his blanket the other day, I thought Woody might actually give in, but no such luck yet. Here's hoping these two don't maim each other with their shenanigans…. My money is on Woody, though. He's a sneaky little crank.

Equine Rule # 36:
No matter how many horse-specific toys you buy...

The joys of horsekeeping. Perhaps I am alone in this, but my horses prefer to play with only the most expensive of items, eschewing all manner of horse-appropriate toys in favor of things like blankets and full water troughs. I've yet to see either touch the Jolly Ball or the little apple thingy with the treat. Jerks. I doubt anyone in the history of riding has had to replace more Jolly Balls than blankets.

Items that are 'OFF LIMITS" will be that much more appealing

Turnout Gear for your Warmblood:

Head bumper:
Protects any potential brain cells (these are few and far between and should be conserved).

Ultra-padded, leather, break-away halter:
Used so that he can free himself from fences or even you if captured (BONUS – then you get a merry chase as a pre-ride warmup)!

Heavy duty protective sheet:
Protects him from sharp pony teeth, his own hooves, parts of the fence he tears down, rain, wind, cold, bugs, and sharp/pokey sticks that only he will find in an otherwise manicured pasture.

Fleece-lined boots:
These have double Velcro with reinforced strike pads to protect the delicate tendons and ligaments he will ultimately try to destroy in his first five minutes out. The hope is that these will *help* prevent any cutting, tearing, ripping, severing, or bludgeoning he can do to ruin his lower legs and ultimately end his career.

Bell boots:
These help keep his uber expensive, corrective special shoes attached to his less than ideal hooves by theoretically preventing him from overreaching and prying them off. They also help prevent him from slicing open his heels and becoming instantly lame. Most likely they will end up off in minutes and become a chew toy.

Because the fancier they are, the quicker they will crash through a fence and experience career-ending injuries. The Quarter Horses, Arabs, ponies, and even OTTBs in my life have all been pretty sane when it comes to turnout. Or at least they don't actively try to die. This has not held true so far for the Warmbloods.

Turnout Gear for ANYTHING Else:

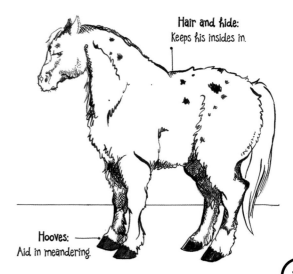

Hair and hide:
Keeps his insides in.

Hooves:
Aid in meandering.

Talking about being hosed…or why you should never trust a hose to be left unattended while on. Really, no matter how well you think you've wedged it in the water trough, it will ultimately prove to you just how precariously perched it actually was. Honestly it wouldn't take much to convince me that they're all actually a little possessed.

Sheath Cleaning:

Normal Geldings:

"Um, this is both awkward and violating. Can we not?"

My Gelding:

"Behold me in ALL my glory! You may proceed."

Yeah… I'm getting a mare next time. I don't have much else to add to this. My horse is a weirdo.

Puddles 101

On the way OUT to turnout:

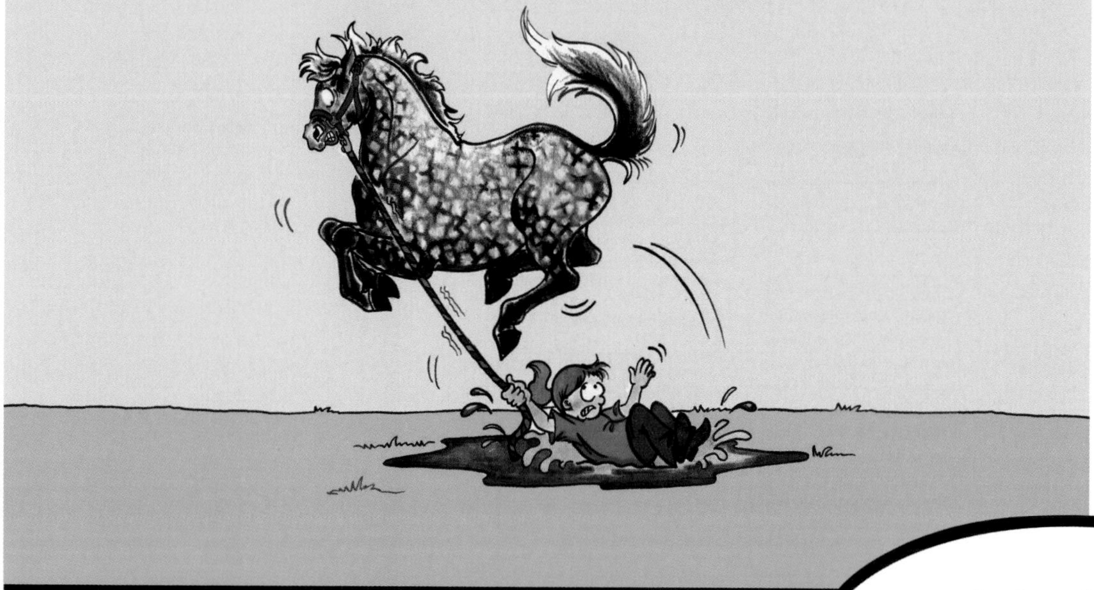

Another sad truth...
I bet you didn't know your horse had Lipizzaner in him, huh? Who doesn't love the daily dose of irony that horses provide?

After being turned out:

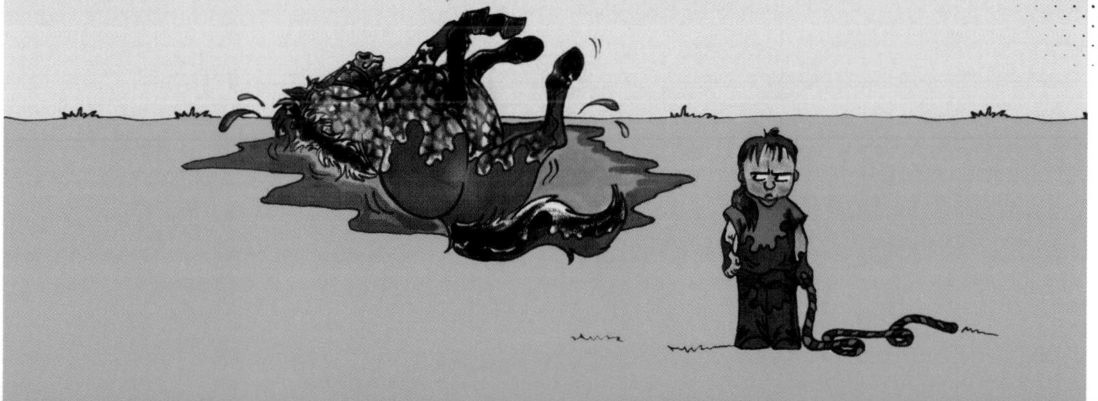

How to Treat your Horse's *Serious* Ailment:

A Flowchart to Success!

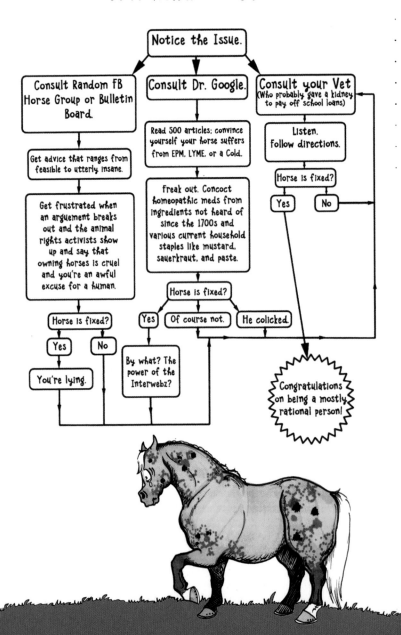

Notice the Issue.

Consult Random FB Horse Group or Bulletin Board.

Get advice that ranges from feasible to utterly insane.

Get frustrated when an argument breaks out and the animal rights activists show up and say that owning horses is cruel and you're an awful excuse for a human.

Horse is fixed?

Yes — No

You're lying.

Consult Dr. Google.

Read 500 articles; convince yourself your horse suffers from EPM, LYME, or a Cold.

freak out. Concoct homeopathic meds from ingredients not heard of since the 1700s and various current household staples like mustard, sauerkraut, and paste.

Horse is fixed?

Yes — Of course not. — He colicked.

By what? The power of the Interwebz?

Consult your Vet
(Who probably gave a kidney to pay off school loans)

Listen. Follow directions.

Horse is fixed?

Yes — No

Congratulations on being a mostly rational person!

Seriously, people. There's a reason we pay vets and not random wackadoos on the internet. So before anyone gets their panties in too tight a bunch, let me preface this by saying I'm actually all for alternative medicines and modalities. I also think that if you can avoid drugs or invasive procedures, then that's probably a good thing. That being said, if there's something seriously sketchy going on with your horse, it's probably best to consult your veterinarian sooner rather than later. If nothing else, it will save you from going insane reading every article on the web about every possible, horrifying thing it *could* be (ask me how I know this).

Entropy, thy Name is 'Warmblood.'

"What did you say his breeding was?

"He's by Grand Apocalypse out of Little Termite."

This is why we can't have nice things. It is also why we need to be independently wealthy. I think we've all had this horse, or at least one who was equally, albeit perhaps differently, destructive. It would seem some horses just find sheer joy in pulling down every fence they can touch and flossing with live hot wire for fun.

Because you don't do enough to support your local vet…. (Can I get a padded stall?) I'm always appreciative when my horses point out the flaws in the craftsmanship of my stalls and fencing; it's so helpful.

"I'm glad you're here early! I think this room has termites; I'd like to request another."

Where would your horse choose to roll?

In the beautiful, spacious, acre paddock free of all debris...

The most cluttered, disaster prone corner with enough panels to stick each foot through a different one...

I swear my two-year-old does this just to watch me squirm. You'd think a prey animal would have a greater aversion to rolling around in a tight space where it might get stuck and become lunch for something higher on the food chain. Alas, this doesn't seem to be how it works.

Yeah, Mine too.

Things you NEVER Want to Hear from your Vet:

"Do you want to hear the good news or the bad news first?"
(Translation: Hooray! It's curable. Boo! You will need to mortgage your house.)

"Let's try some more blocks."
(Translation: Yeah, this is going to be more involved than we'd hoped.)

"I'm surprised to say the scope showed no ulcers..."
(Translation: Your horse is such a turd even I thought it had to be more than just his personality.)

"Hmm, interesting..."
(Translation: You're about to go down a very expensive rabbit hole.)

"Well, he's lame, but not lame enough to diagnose anything. Keep working him and see if it gets worse."
(Translation: You need to make him more lame so I can come back and we can do another lameness exam.)

"Wow, I've only read about this!"
(Translation: You're SOL on this one.)

Things you'd rather not hear from your vet. Ever. I think if you've been in horses longer than a minute, you've had your fair share of less-than-fun conversations with your vet. While logic might have you think the most upsetting things would involve horrendous maiming or death, the reality is that the unknown ambiguity is far more terrifying (and expensive). While it's never amusing when your horse is hurt, you have to admit there's a bit of humor in the terror certain seemingly innocuous phrases can induce in us. Anyone care to share their own?

Sounds like a GREAT plan...
Because I'm sure this is a totally
reasonable request...
I admit to pulling my horses' manes–
mostly because the resulting braids
seem to be far better–but I can't
help but think they're getting
the shaft in that scenario.

"So, let me get this straight, you want me to stand
here quietly while you use a metal comb to rip my
hair out by the roots?

Oh sure, sounds great. You go right ahead with that.
I'll just stand here and plot your untimely demise."

44

Signs Your Horse Might be Passive Aggressive:

When Lunch is 15 Minutes Late

We know there can be,
at times, a propensity for passive-aggressive
drama in the equestrian community (but
certainly never brought on by any of us...). I would
also argue that certain equine beasts
I know have demonstrated
this particular trait.

My favorite activity…. If you're doing it at ALL, you're doing it wrong. Have you ever noticed how things never turn out like the picture? This holds true for things you cook, assemble, or find on Pinterest. Just give it up now; acceptance is key. Of course, my less than stellar clip job is probably more a reflection of my laziness and less of my inability to wield clippers. Every year I swear I will wash the pony, wait for him to dry, coat him in show sheen, and then clip correctly, and EVERY year I randomly get fed up with his hair and opt to clip it RIGHT then (sans bath or any other worthwhile prep). The results are about what you'd expect: cold, angry pony with random tufts of fuzz and clipper tracks. Ah, well, there's always next time…

Body Clipping:

You're Doing it Wrong.

"I don't care if you look like Hannibal Lector, it's for your own good."

The grass is always greener on the other side of a muzzle. It's springtime– okay, well, sort of. Yesterday I woke up to snow and nearly cried; thankfully, it melted off by noon. In any event, even in the desert spring means diet time for Woody, who apparently can take nutritive content from the air (it's his special talent). As you might imagine, he's not pleased. I'm hoping he can quell his homicidal urges.

"So, are we clipping flirt like Woody?"

"No, I was thinking of trying a 'trace clip.'"

"Oh. What's that? Have you done that before?"

"No. But look. It's fancier. And I don't have to clip as much."

"Hmm, it looks cool. Maybe hard to get even though."

...

"I mean...how hard can it be?"

Karma? Despite telling myself I wasn't going to clip Flirt–in order to save myself the potential death and dismemberment that may ensue once the temperature drops and he gets a cool breeze under his tail–I just couldn't take his fuzziness. As a sort of compromise, I decided to try a trace clip; in theory, he'd be less fuzzy, but he wouldn't get as much of a chill (as an added bonus, I also wouldn't have to clip as much). Having never done a trace clip and only really having a vague idea of what one looked like, I decided to Google it for a picture. This resulted in a plethora of "trace clip" pictures but no discernible pattern that might hint at which photo actually showed a correct clip. At this point I figured it probably didn't matter, said screw it, and made up my own…. While it went well enough, I did fail to consider the amount of thought involved in getting the damn thing even. The final results? Somewhat dodgy.

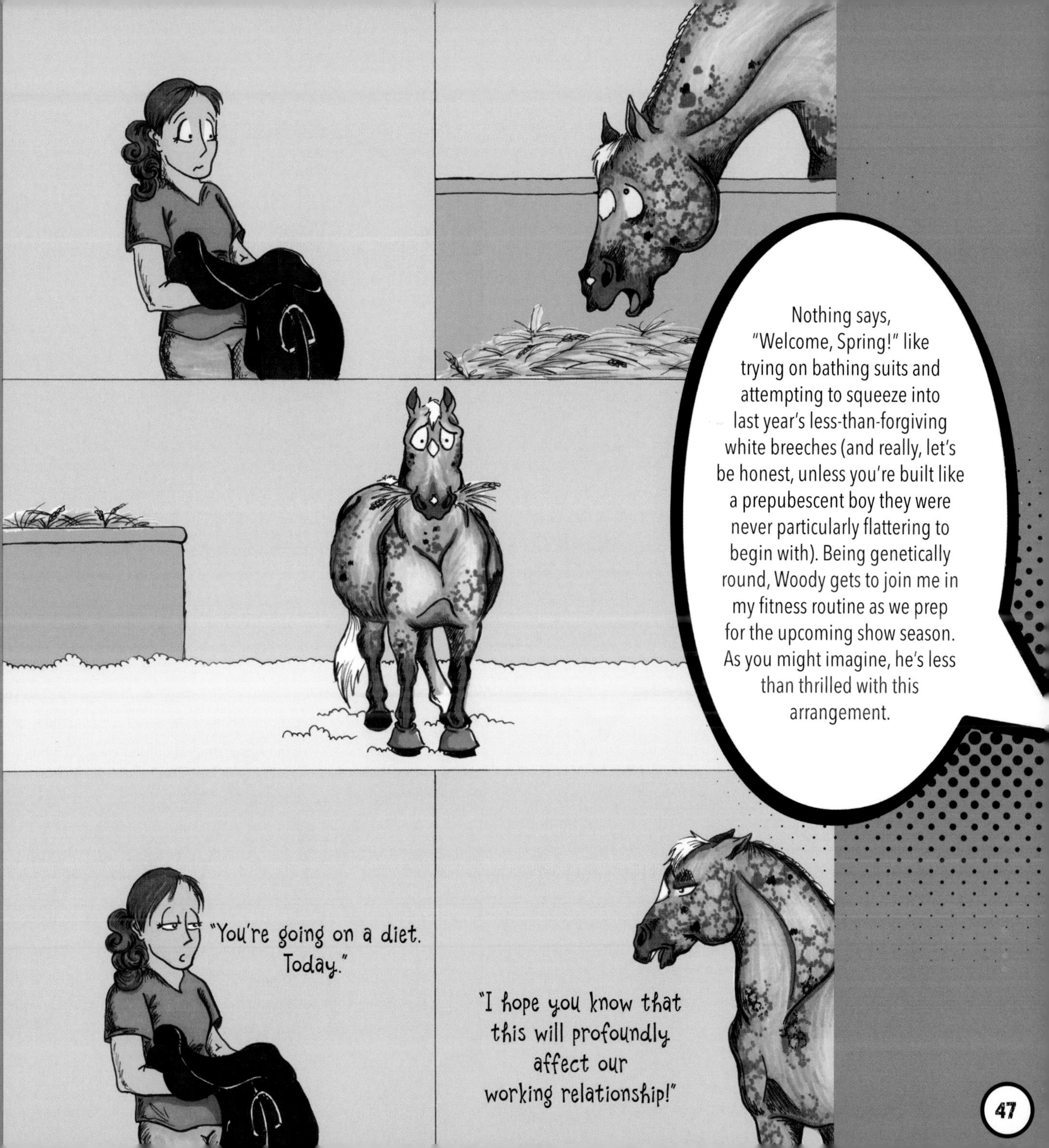
Nothing says, "Welcome, Spring!" like trying on bathing suits and attempting to squeeze into last year's less-than-forgiving white breeches (and really, let's be honest, unless you're built like a prepubescent boy they were never particularly flattering to begin with). Being genetically round, Woody gets to join me in my fitness routine as we prep for the upcoming show season. As you might imagine, he's less than thrilled with this arrangement.
"You're going on a diet. Today."
"I hope you know that this will profoundly affect our working relationship!"

One Way to Make Body Clipping More *Interesting*
(But no less tragic)

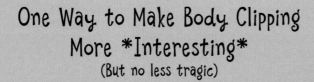

"I don't care if you saw it on the INTERWEBZ! This is an abomination!"

The "Pinterest Clip"… No less tragic indeed. As soon as I clip once, I begin to fear Round Two. Let the doom of the season come upon us.

That moment that the realization dawns on you…. Anyone else have a horse like this? I swear both my unfortunately colored horses think they're playing some warped variation of Twister whenever a hose comes near.

"I KNOW that YOU KNOW EXACTLY what you're doing!"

"Well, it took $80.00 in diesel, 90 miles each way, 7 hours, copious painkillers, and a bit of bloodshed **BUT** we managed to save $0.32 a bale!"

Math involving horses is often…fuzzy. Why do I always forget just how AWFUL this activity is until I am doing it again? Anything to save a few bucks, right?

"Seriously, could you maybe go 24 hours without destroying something expensive or yourself?!"

This is life with a baby Warmblood. I suppose if I am honest, it's life with nearly any horse you love, because if you didn't love them, you'd kill them.

Maybe this is just me, but….there's nothing like the smell of hay and manure in the morning. Really. There isn't. So, while I completely believe that mucking stalls when you HAVE to, or are in some sort of time crunch (like I am 99 percent of the time), is a totally wretched experience, I do find that there is something relaxing about stall-cleaning when there's no pressure. Despite my hatred for mornings, I especially enjoy picking stalls early when it's just the horses and me at the barn. Yet another example that confirms we horse people are a special kind of crazy.

Further Proof that my Horse has it Better than Most People…

Room Service Twice a Day

Daily Maid Service

Daily Massage

Daily Adoration

Equestrian Guilty Pleasure #14:

Cleaning stalls when you have all the time in the world to do so.

Of course, this just further solidifies the fact that my horses should behave themselves for the 45 minutes a day I ask them to actually "do" something.

SEASONS ARE FUN

(Except for Winter)

The last chapter covered the general entropy horses bring about, but there are additional challenges unique to each season one must consider. Being originally from Florida, where we have only two seasons—"Monsoon" and "On Fire"—I was particularly well-suited to cope with those associated with humidity, bugs, and heat stroke. I was NOT, however, prepared for the utter horror that is winter. Seriously, there's not enough wine and polar fleece in the world to make it okay (Pro Tip: In the winter, today's spilled water bucket is tomorrow's black-ice death trap. Who knew?) This chapter will familiarize you with common seasonal challenges for equestrians as well as my delightful attitude toward all things winter-related.

Riding in the Summer...

"I'm heading to the barn."

"Ok, what time will you be back?"

"Umm... I shouldn't be long."

"...So... before Fall then? You'll be back before Fall?"

"Well duh! I'd need a jacket by then."

Summer riding... truly an odyssey of sorts. It's easy to lose track of time when the sun is shining and there's a lack of that white doom on the ground.

Riding in July:
The Negotiations Begin

"You're kidding, right?"

I make it a policy that I can only complain about one season at a time because otherwise it's just absurd. Obviously, my intense hatred for all things cold and snowy means that I will never be complaining about summer and its 100+ temperatures. Of course, that doesn't stop everyone else around me.

Why, hello, Summer!
Thanks for bringing your friends
Heat Stroke and Sweaty Butt
with you!

Equestrians:
Never Satisfied

Last Week:

"I am SO Over freezing!
Where is Summer?!"

This Week:

"This heat is RIDICULOUS!
I can't wait for Summer
to be OVER!"

Another Sign That Summer is Dead,
WINTER IS COMING:
Cool Mornings and Alarmed Warmbloods

"What is your deal?
Are you seriously
spooking at Breakfast?!"

"Let it be known that you are literally
spooking at the hand that feeds you...
Every.Single.Day."

"You just keep doing you, buddy."

As much as I have to
admit that I could "survive" without
it being over 100 degrees outside, I am NOT
too thrilled about fall shenanigans (or the doom that
comes after it). At least all my horses are enjoying
spooking at their own shadows for funsies.

"Seriously? It's only September."

·WINTER is coming!·

This is blasphemy to some, but I am not a pumpkin-scented-flavored-colored fan. So, really, there's not a whole lot awesome about the fall time of year. (Except Halloween; I love Halloween.) But seriously, though– here's to surviving the doom we know is to come…

I'm not sure what sense there is behind horses shedding right before they grow in their winter coat. I mean, really, it seems to me that it'd be more energy efficient to just add a bit more hair to what's already there. In any event, it is a telltale sign that summer is coming to a close and I am dreading the inevitable cold (and FYI cold is anything below 50 degrees).

Fall Approaches...

"Seriously? It's a decoration!"

"Festive Orange DOOM-Squash!"

May your pumpkin be spicy and your horse mild.

DOOM-O-LANTERN
The slightly more terrifying cousin of the Festive Doom Squash.

"It breathes FIRE?!"

"Makes you appreciate the Festive Doom Squash, huh?"

Not only are Festive Doom Squashes a no-go, turns out their flaming Doom-O-Lantern cousins are also harbingers of death (for you rather than your horse).

It's Fall: Time for Pumpkin EVERYTHING

"Hello, Small Predator! Being that it's Fall, I'd like to request **pumpkin spice hay** for lunch this afternoon...your previous offering was subpar. Ok, thanks."

A sign of the times? Or just the epitome of first-world problems? Perhaps you're one of the billions who loves the onslaught of pumpkin-spice-flavored ANYTHING. I myself am NOT a huge fan, but I am highly amused at the divide something as insignificant as coffee syrup can cause.

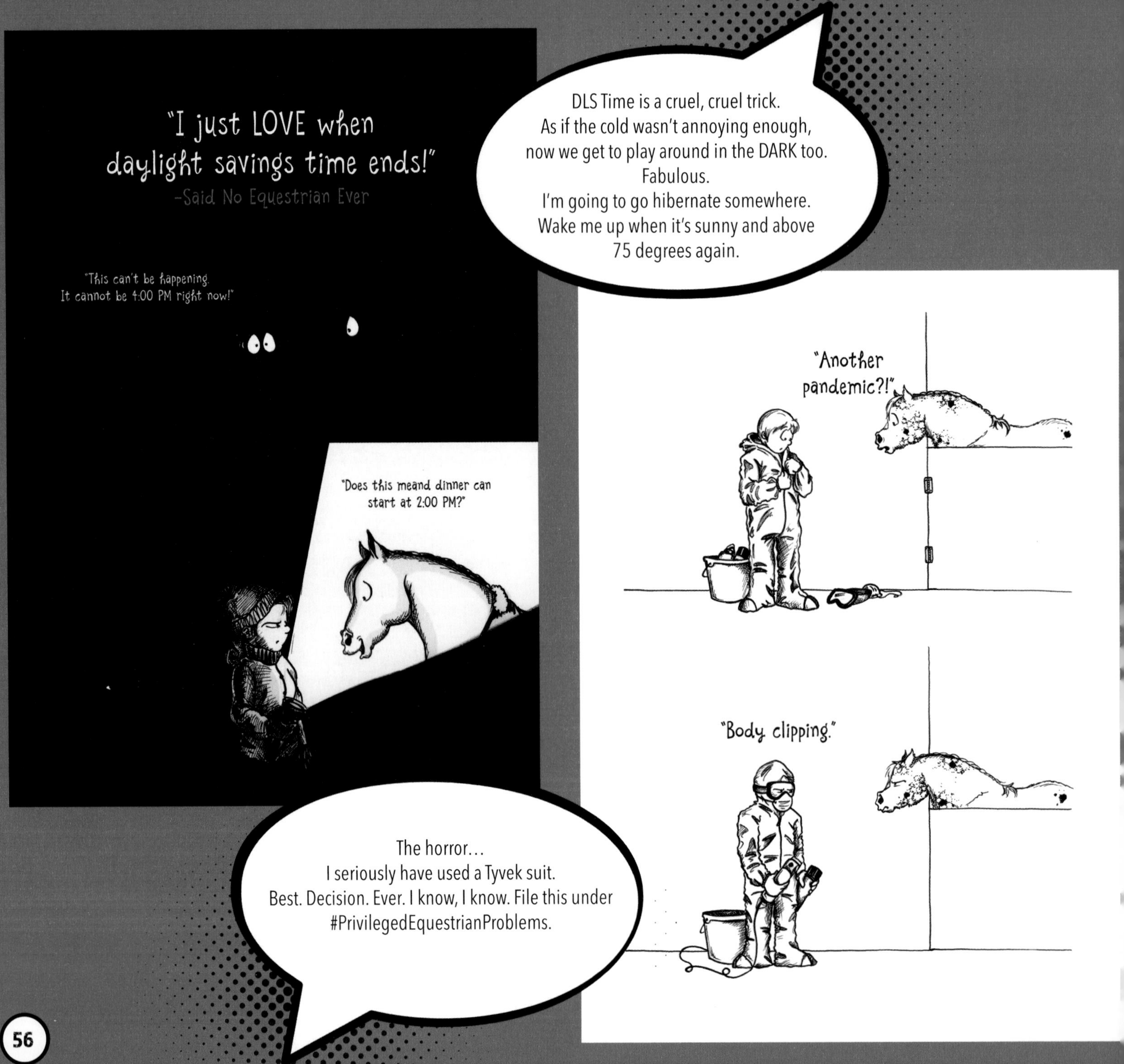
"I just LOVE when daylight savings time ends!"
-Said No Equestrian Ever
"This can't be happening. It cannot be 4:00 PM right now!"
"Does this meand dinner can start at 2:00 PM?"
DLS Time is a cruel, cruel trick. As if the cold wasn't annoying enough, now we get to play around in the DARK too. Fabulous. I'm going to go hibernate somewhere. Wake me up when it's sunny and above 75 degrees again.
"Another pandemic?!"
"Body clipping."
The horror… I seriously have used a Tyvek suit. Best. Decision. Ever. I know, I know. File this under #PrivilegedEquestrianProblems.

60-minute ride?
Not unless you have staff.
Or only if you start with almost
twice that amount of time.
This is one of the
things that is mildly
annoying about fall—it's an
awkward time of year where the
grooming load increases,
riding schedules get spotty due
to random weather patterns,
and your horse is just starting
to notice the brisk air.
All this while daylight decreases.
Also, it means winter—
so there's that.

60 Minutes of "Riding": FALL EDITION

Grooming
35 mins

Because your horse has suddenly become a yak and the freak snow storm the day before has melted (because it isn't *real* winter yet) turning everything into muck which is now cemented to your yak. Oh, and also because he will be a sweaty mess before you even get on him due to his yakness and the awkwardly warm temps so you'll need at least 15 minutes at the end to groom him.

Catching
10 mins

Because he will be somewhere in the back 40 due to being stoked at finally being turned out again after the wet weather.

Lunging
10 mins

Because the brisk air and spotty riding schedule will transform your otherwise sedate beast into a snorty dragon.

Riding
5 mins

Because who wanted to do that anyway, right?

Fall…. More a verb than a noun these days.
So, this morning was apparently the first real morning of fall and no one was pleased. If I were bright, I'd have followed my own advice and de-boarded.
Instead, I pressed on and rode through an impressive array of shenanigans. One of these days I'll learn to make better life choices.

Body Clipping:
Taking you one step closer to insanity.

"You know, sometimes I wonder about you."

"It isn't my fault you don't know great art when you see it."

The First 30° Morning...

"So...are you riding this morning?"

"Nope. The biggest Nope that ever Noped."

Just one of the MANY insane things we do as equestrians. The one where we get to be covered in hair AND eventually freeze in the ensuing arctic tundra. Barf. I'm already ready for June.

Winter is Still Here:
Desperate times call for desperate measures...

"What are you doing?"

"Trying to find the arena."

"That cold, huh?"

"Shut it. *LOOKS GOOD WITH DOBBIN! STRETCH UP AND DROP INTO YOUR HEELS...*"

"Umm... That blanket smells like pee."

"Hush. Did you get coffee yet?! *NICE. EYES UP. LOOKS GOOOOOD...*"

Winter as...desperation?
The season brings out all sorts of things in people. Some are excited by the clean freshness that seems to come with newly fallen snow. These people are joyous at what they perceive to be new beginnings and boundless possibilities. I am not these people. Winter brings out nothing in me but acute depression and irritability.

When your Horse has a Sense of Humor...

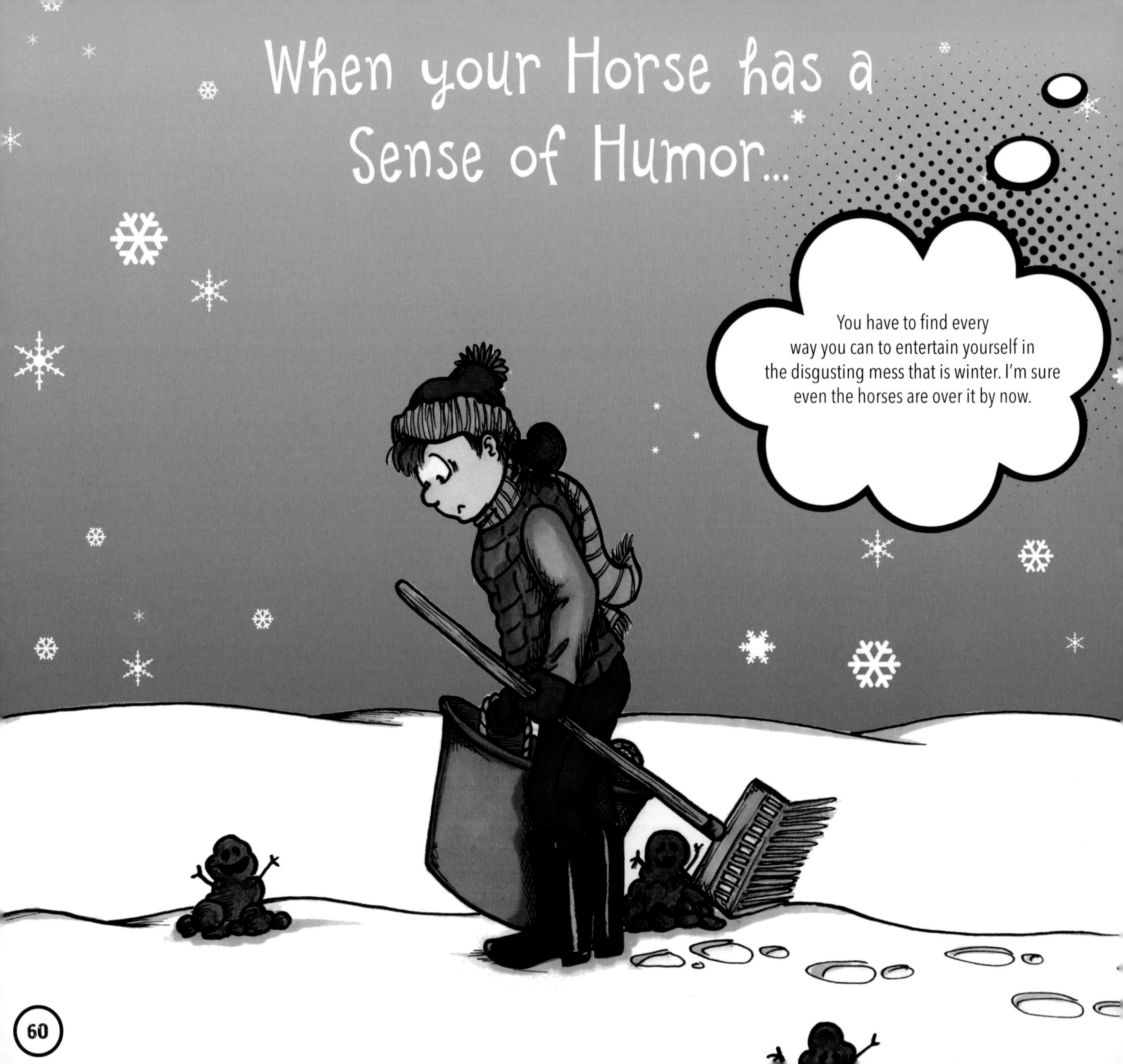
You have to find every way you can to entertain yourself in the disgusting mess that is winter. I'm sure even the horses are over it by now.

Things I Like About Winter:
A Comprehensive List

In an attempt to foster a more positive outlook, I have decided to make a list of the favorable aspects of winter.

1._____

IT ENDS

Well, I gave it a shot. At least there's only another four-ish months of this sacrilege.

Ah, snow…destroyer of my endless summer dreams. By now you know my feelings on winter and snow. But, just in case you've forgotten, here's a reminder.

SNOW
How Non-Horse People See It:

How Horse People See It:

Be kind…and maybe come help break some ice buckets and shovel a few tons of snow. Because snow-induced homicidal rage is a real thing. I think I speak for everyone who owns livestock in a cold climate when I say, "Enough is ENOUGH, already!"

Hello, Winter.
We meet again.

PSA: Be Kind to your Equestrian Friends this Winter;
THEY'RE NOT DOING WELL.

It might be time for those trough heaters… Yes, hello, Winter, you creep. Isn't it time for you to leave yet? It's officially here when you have to break ice off the water troughs in the mornings. The other day, I wrote my name in the snow with Stormy's hoofprints during our warmup. I guess that was fun.

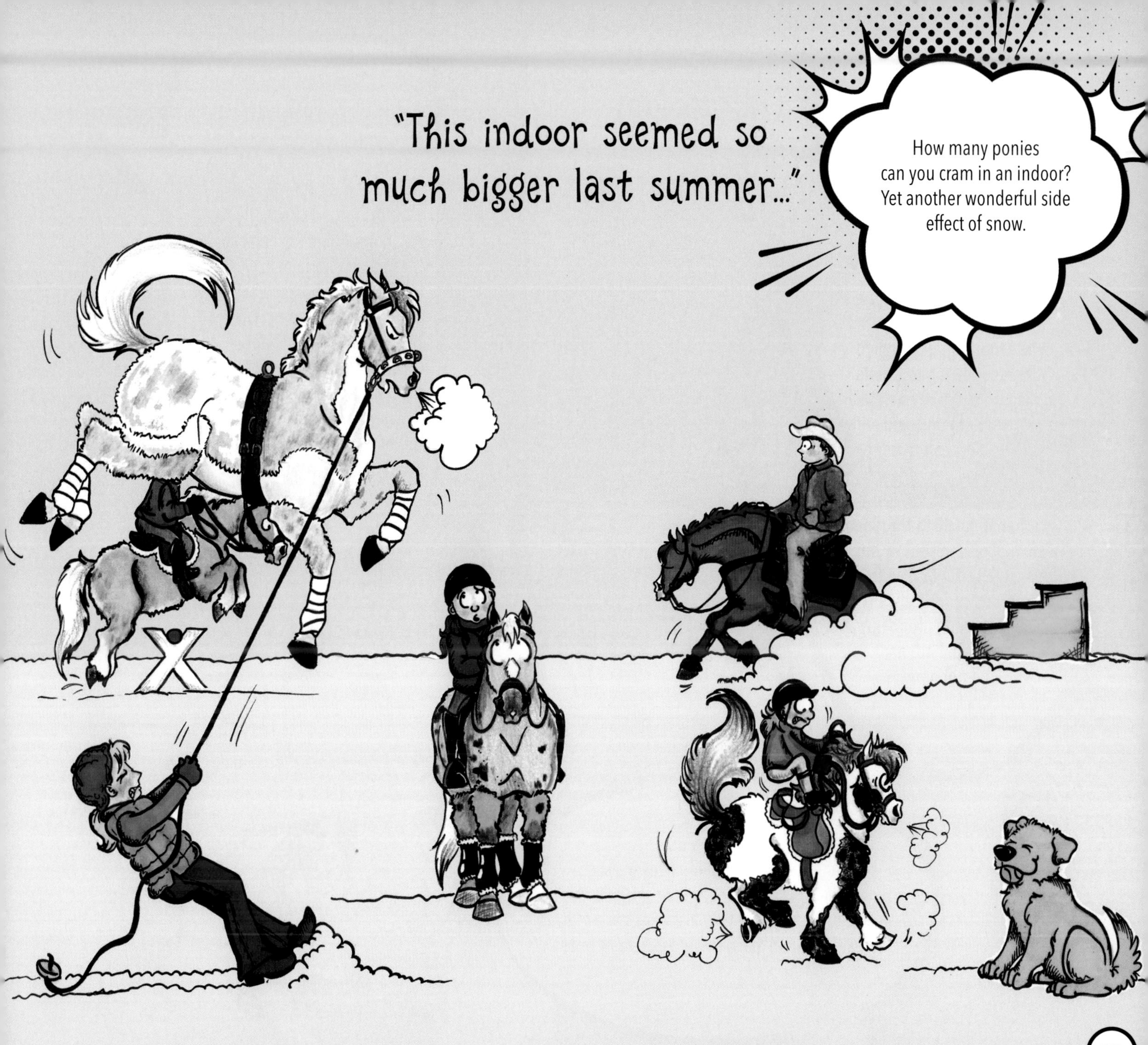
"This indoor seemed so much bigger last summer..."
How many ponies can you cram in an indoor? Yet another wonderful side effect of snow.

My horse after I dress him in 47 layers...

"Should I assume you're cold, Small Predator?"

I feel like this is what my horse is saying to me every time I go to throw yet another blanket on him. Of course, I'm fairly certain that nine times out of ten I blanket him according to how cold I feel instead of what's likely more appropriate for a 1,200-pound hairball. This tendency is, of course, exacerbated by the fact that I'm from Florida (a land free of winter bogusness) and think anything below 70 degrees is uncivilized.

TIME SAVING OR JUST TORTURE?

He has a point...
Although I'd like to think my beasts understand why I have shorn their yak pelts this last week, I'm fairly certain they just think I'm a sadistic monster bent on making them miserably frozen.

"Body clipping sure saves a ton of time on grooming!"

"Yes, and I'm sure going NAKED would save you a TON of time on laundry but I don't see you freezing your bum off!"

Reason #17 that
EQUESTRIANS WINTER IN FLORIDA

I call shenanigans on this winter BS. The next person who tells me to think positively when it's -9 degrees outside is getting a face full of snow.

Ah, Winter,
"I'm SO glad it's a high of 15 degrees today, so that I can practice my Airs Above the Ground..."

Said No One EVER.

Winter 'Riding'
The ultimate preparation for summer water skiing.

The Joys of Winter Abound.

Hurricanes?
Sissy stuff. Those are WARM!
Here we have FROZEN CYCLONES.
You're welcome.
Love, Winter.

Another SHOCKING Reason
Winter is Terrible....

Shocking indeed…coming from Florida,
where the average humidity is like 110 percent, the
whole "static electricity thing" was somewhat foreign
to me. Rest assured, though, that I'm now quite
familiar with it and have added it (along with the
trauma it brings my young, less-than-stoic Warmblood)
to my myriad list of reasons that winter is worthless.

"Oh, right. Like I enjoy this any
more than you do."

Poopcicles...

Just one more of Winter's
sparkling treasures.

clink, clink

A Wonderland indeed...
I wonder how many damn muck rakes
I'll break before the thaw hits.

So it
snowed again...
Have I mentioned how
much I hate snow? I hate
watching my horses nearly
break their fetlocks
even more.

"I'm calling the farrier."

"KILLJOY."

A legit question…
though one most may not appreciate
you asking. Ah, winter and the holidays: a time of
wonderfully frozen tundra complete with copious amounts
of food and significantly less motivation to do much other
than eat it. It's a time of wonderment: Is your horse just
fluffy from being frozen or fat from not getting worked?
Do those breeches feel snug because you layered
or because you've decided pumpkin pie is a
legitimate food group? So. Many. Questions.

It's that time of year...

"Are you FAT or
just fluffy?!"

"Do we REALLY
want to go there,
KAREN?!"

In Devastating News:
WINTER IS STILL HERE.

"Seriously?"

"I made you a snowman to
cheer you up about winter."

"Thanks! I feel much better."

"Do you want to build a
snowman?" Do I LOOK like I wanna do
anything with snow? In no uncertain terms: NEVER.
Even though it's only January, I have fully reached
my limit regarding my tolerance for winter. If it
had a face, I probably would take just a little too
much glee from melting it.

Musical Blankets? A game no one wins. You know what I *love*? Trying to decipher which of the 47 blankets is best suited for the greatest amount of time on any given day (because playing Musical Blankets is highly overrated). And yet it never fails—the days seem to go from arctic tundra directly into sweltering hot mess.

Blanketing Fun:
It's That Time of Year...

8:59 AM

9:01 AM

Top 15 Things Equestrians Google in January:

1. Can your brain cells freeze together?
2. How many days left until spring?
3. Best price for bulk ordering foot warmers
4. Best deal on bulk coffee
5. Best way to unfreeze your truck door
6. Can I salt my horse's paddock?
7. Weed torch to thaw driveway ice?
8. Best deal on bulk wine
9. Xanax dosing
10. What's the best calming 'supplement'?
11. What's the most durable lunge line?
12. Lunging with a winch--too much?
13. How much wine is too much to go riding?
14. Boarding costs in Florida
15. Cost to build an indoor arena

I have Googled all of these….
There may have been some searches involving "nearest ER" and "low-cost fares to Hawaii," as well. But seriously, though—I've gone through all of these. Good thing the weather has been so crummy as it has allowed me time to thoroughly explore them, as well as re-familiarize myself with the sad fact that I'll never be rich enough to build an indoor.

When you horse has access to a
PERFECTLY GOOD STALL
but still chooses to hang outside in the blizzard...

Because who needs shelter, warmth, and a perfectly dry stall when you have an entire wet, frozen tundra at your disposal?

"Surely you don't think this is MY fault?!"

The *FUN* after the snow storm...

It's sNOw fun.... Never. Not even a little bit. It's hard to deny that attempting to clean snow-covered paddocks is not even remotely amusing. Well, not for the person cleaning, anyhow. My horses all seem pretty pleased with themselves, and the bystanders at the barn apparently get a kick out of my ability to string together unique combinations of profanities—so there's that.

"Good morning, Favorite Human!

I know how much you love scavenger hunts so I made sure to do ALL my business before the snow was done.

You're welcome.

I also may have hidden both front shoes and a brush you left unfortunately close to my stall door."

Pony Apocalypse. (Never trust a pony.)

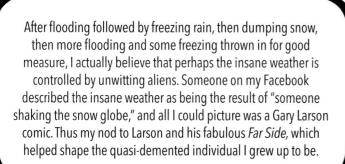

"I know what you're thinking; it looks like the work of zombies to me too! I've already phoned the CDC."

IT ALL MAKES SENSE NOW...

"Seriously? What's the deal?"

"Someone shook the snow globe again."

After flooding followed by freezing rain, then dumping snow, then more flooding and some freezing thrown in for good measure, I actually believe that perhaps the insane weather is controlled by unwitting aliens. Someone on my Facebook described the insane weather as being the result of "someone shaking the snow globe," and all I could picture was a Gary Larson comic. Thus my nod to Larson and his fabulous *Far Side,* which helped shape the quasi-demented individual I grew up to be.

SNUD:
ALL THE DISGUSTING PROPERTIES OF BOTH SNOW & MUD!

"Seriously?"

"Hi, favorite Human!
I love the
glorious SNUD!
It exfoliates AND
ensures that you small
predators give adequate
massages.
It's very therapeutic."

It's time for one
of my favorite things…Just kidding.
I also hate this too. What's even more annoying
and gross than snow? SNUD! The hybrid
snow-mud sludge that turns your horse (and pasture,
arena, driveway, yard–basically all it touches) into a
cold, soppy, crusty, dirty mess. This is one of
Winter's lovely parting gifts.

Spring is here…and she's a GIANT
tease! Well, she pops in for a moment or two,
anyhow. I must say I find it thoroughly depressing to
be frolicking in the 70-degree sunshine one day only to
wake up to yet another Snowmageddon the next.
Ugh. I totally understand why people give up on
seasons and move to Florida.

Spring is Here!

SUNDAY:

"The sun is out, the flowers are blooming and
I AM WEARING SHORT SLEEVES!
Today is AWESOME!"

MONDAY:

"If you need me, I'll be in the house listening
to my soul slowly die."

Spring is Coming!

"I've got no sympathy kid;
you're the one who's been complaining
about winter."

"Aren't you SO excited
that Spring is here, Small Predator?"

Transitions are hard…on every level. On horses and between seasons. While I am incredibly relieved that spring is on the way and there's an end in sight to the cold misery that is winter, I could seriously do without the mud, snud, and hair. I'm also hating the last-minute storms Winter tosses at me in one final attempt at ruining my life.

Spring Cleaning:
BECAUSE SPIDERS DON'T CLEAR THEMSELVES OUT.

Did you know at any given moment you're 8 feet from a spider? I may, in fact, be the only one who has had the pleasure of cleaning those "little white things" under the rims of the water buckets, only to unleash an unholy Hell upon myself in the form of hundreds of baby arachnids. But then again, perhaps I'm not. For those lucky enough to have avoided this, do yourself a favor and ask your younger sibling to take care of the buckets.

The lousy part of spring is that it sometimes still snows. Oh, and there are bugs again. Those suck. Please tell me I'm not alone in thinking that most fly-spray is an expensive joke? I'm especially amused by the claim that it lasts multiple days. Seriously?

"Can we all just take a moment and agree that that spray is useless?!"

CHALLENGE ACCEPTED

(Why Training Isn't for the Faint of Heart)

If you manage to keep your horse alive and mostly sound and happy, odds are some sort of training will be part of the picture. There is more nuance to "horse training" than an entire library could cover, but all you really need to know is that whatever level you're on will be absurdly, ridiculously harder and more time-consuming than you would ever believe possible. In particular, dressage training never actually gets any easier, and, in fact, the more you learn, and the more "trained" your horse becomes, the more you realize just how woefully inadequate you are. It's okay, though, at least your fellow riders are there for you (and are not at all judgmental about your riding, training, saddle pad color, or bit selection). And, thankfully, you also have this awesome book to enlighten you about some of the training challenges horses and riders face as they work their way up the levels.

EQUINE 'SHOWER THOUGHTS:"

"What if the small predators aren't just annoying when they're up there kicking and pulling, what if they're TRYING TO COMMUNICATE?!"

"What?"

Naa. They're not that advanced."

"Yeah, you're probably right."

So, for those unfamiliar with what a shower thought is, feel free to hit up Reddit. A brief and perhaps telling example would be the following exchange with a friend:
Me: "What if the crazy people who hear voices aren't *really* crazy, but are just tuned into a different dimension or something that we don't hear?" Friend: "......"
Me: "What? I'm not saying they're NOT crazy....just...I dunno, maybe they aren't?...." Friend: (Slowly walks away)

You know that moment, the one right before something awful happens with your horse when you're thinking, "Hmm, this could go poorly," and yet you fail to react? Yeah, I know it too. And it usually is over something absurdly silly. Of course, in this specific scenario the rodent likely latches onto the horse's nose and causes enough trauma to justify all sorts of future spooking.

"Don't touch that- you'll scare yourself."

There is little doubt that we see the world a bit differently than our equine companions, though given their reactions sometimes I do question just how differently that must be…. In my experience, horses also seem to see boogie men in drainage ditches, garbage cans, mail boxes, and most shadowy areas. Maybe they know something we don't?

Social distancing... your horse's new favorite thing.

If my horse was aware that
SOCIAL DISTANCING
was a thing...

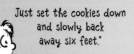

"STOP!
Um, I'm pretty sure that you riding me does NOT follow the established SOCIAL DISTANCING PROTOCOL.

Just set the cookies down and slowly back away six feet."

Different Perspectives
SOME ARE MORE RATIONAL THAN OTHERS

WHAT YOU SEE: WHAT YOUR HORSE SEES:

Common plastic bag

Death from above

Small ditch

Pit of doom and certain death

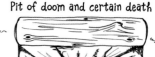

Small woodland creature

CLOSE UP OF WOODLAND FOE

Blood thirsty, horse destroying monster of unknown origin

Communication...
CAN BE DIFFICULT

"What's wrong?"

"I think my horse is an idiot! I take him to the base of the jump and he just darts or dives around it! He JUST DOESN'T GET IT. Why does he make things SO DIFFICULT?!"

"What's wrong?"

"I think my rider is an idiot! She keeps steering me into small walls and then gets upset when I get us around them! She's JUST NOT WITH IT. Why does she make things SO DIFFICULT?!"

Is it even possible to truly understand each other? While I'm certain I'd rather not have to hear how measly their rations are or how they'd prefer not to work today thank-you-very-much, it would be nice if we could just explain to them verbally exactly what we're trying to get them to do. I'm sure it would clear up quite a bit for all of us involved.

"Embrace the Suck."
Because it is actually an integral part of training. Training horses is a truly rewarding endeavor… except, of course, when it's not. But those sucky moments are all part of the challenge that helps us grow, both as people and equestrians, so I suppose we should embrace them (a shout-out to Lauren Sprieser for coining this oh-so-apt phrase).

TRAINER DISCUSSIONS:

"While I realize you're young, I think it'd be prudent for you to realize that the sooner you suck it up and act like a civilized beast, the sooner you'll get a nice amateur lady who will give you cookies and supplements and acupuncture.
Until then, it's just you and me."

Texts Your Trainer Could Probably Live Without

The joys of text messages…how we pretend to communicate while not ACTUALLY communicating. I am a HUGE fan of text messaging, particularly because I'm always overbooked and running around like my hair is on fire. I rarely check my voicemail (and by rarely I mean, "I have voicemail?") so texting is really the best way to get ahold of me. That being said, some text messages–while quasi-convenient– are perhaps best left unsent.

11:53 PM

Hi! I found a flysheet for Dobbin that I really like but it comes in blue plaid and yellow plaid. I think he'd look lovely in the blue but the yellow is kinda daring, you know. What do you think?

...it's almost midnight....on a Sunday.

Ok... so blue or yellow?

I want to order before midnight to save the 10%.

11:57 PM

Seriously. This is IMPORTANT!
11:57 PM

Friday, Jun 8 • 1:00 PM

Hi! I bought the mare; you're going to LOVE her!

What mare is this?

The pretty one.

You mean the lame one!?

The breeder assured me she'll be sound. Xrays are just a guide anyway.
Besides, she's BEAUTIFUL!

'Lame' is so subjective anyway.
Jun 8, 1:05 PM

10:10 PM

Hey, so remember how we talked about turning my two geldings out together?

Um, yes? I said that was probably not a good plan since they both have shoes...

Yeah, so they both still have shoes on and there's only a moderate amount of bleeding... but I may need to cancel lessons this week.
10:12 PM

386-881-2110

10:16 PM

hi, i am interested in horse riding. i saw your fb page. i have done some pony rides when i was younger so i think i am pretty skilled. i was wondering if you had a horse i could take on rides around the area. i would be good exercise for your horse. i would only adk a small fee for my time. maybe $20? lmk, k? thx
10:16 PM

Early Morning Conversations with your Horse:

"Could you just go around today with your back up and stay IN the ring?!"

"Um. Yeah. I'm gonna need to discuss amongst myself. I'll get back to you."

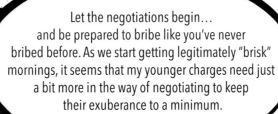

Let the negotiations begin… and be prepared to bribe like you've never bribed before. As we start getting legitimately "brisk" mornings, it seems that my younger charges need just a bit more in the way of negotiating to keep their exuberance to a minimum.

That Moment When...

Regardless of your equine prowess, things quickly degenerate into Amateur Hour.

Because tying an 1,100-pound animal to a string and holding on is a great idea.... Does this seem foolish to anyone else? Seriously? No matter how much I learn, there are still those humbling moments with horses when I feel like a real schmuck.

Just a thought…and yet people are still paying $46.60 for one of these gems (unless they already sold their soul for a membership–then they only have to pay $34.95). I'm not against "Natural Horsemanship"... but I am baffled by how expensive it is. Does anyone else find this ironic?

No one ever went to the Olympics by shaking a 'carrot stick' at a warmblood. Just sayin'.

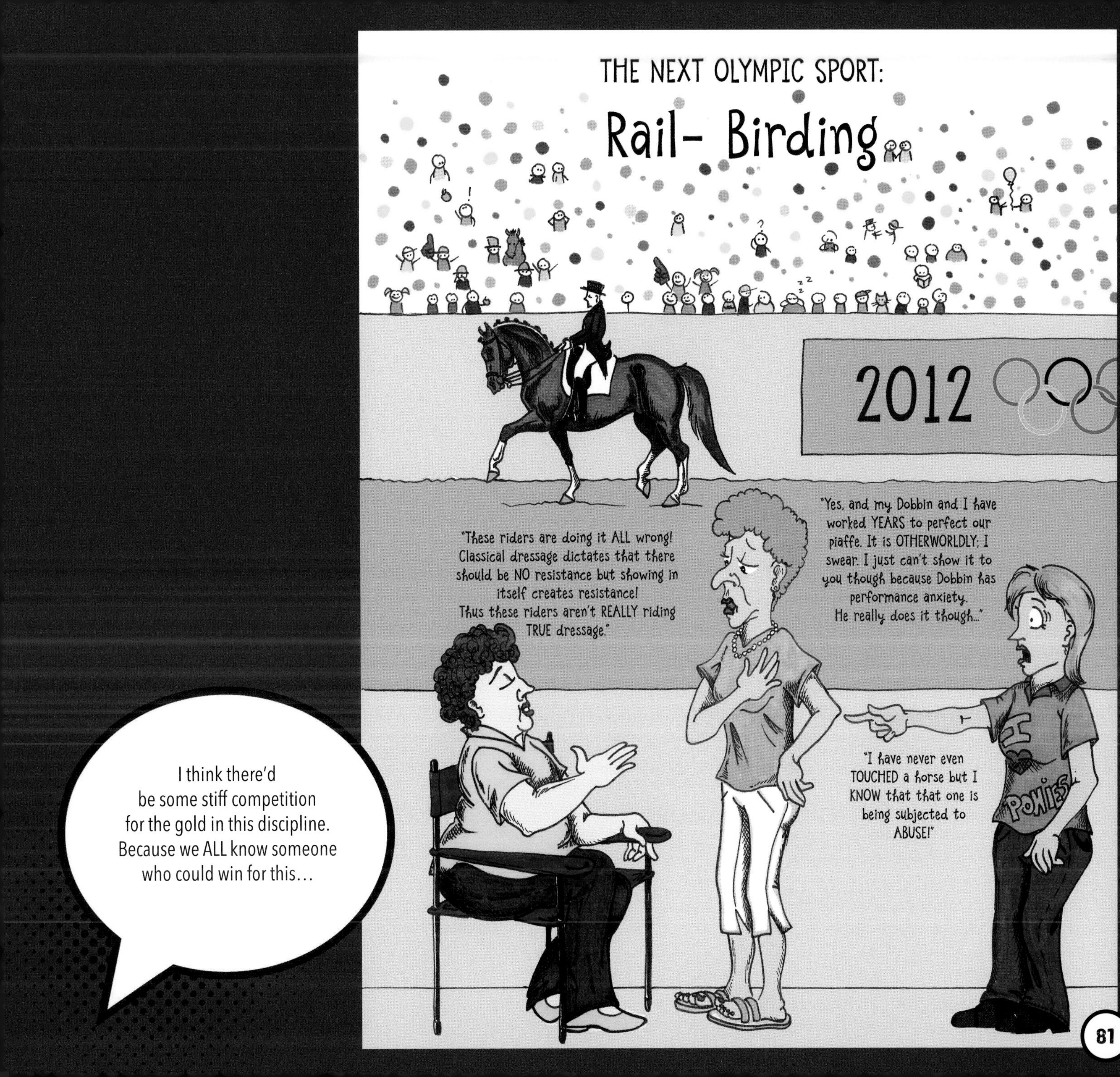

THE NEXT OLYMPIC SPORT:
Rail- Birding
2012
"These riders are doing it ALL wrong! Classical dressage dictates that there should be NO resistance but showing in itself creates resistance! Thus these riders aren't REALLY riding TRUE dressage."
"Yes, and my Dobbin and I have worked YEARS to perfect our piaffe. It is OTHERWORLDLY; I swear. I just can't show it to you though because Dobbin has performance anxiety. He really does it though..."
"I have never even TOUCHED a horse but I KNOW that that one is being subjected to ABUSE!"
PONIES

I think there'd be some stiff competition for the gold in this discipline. Because we ALL know someone who could win for this…

I think we've all been here. At least when I am royally failing at some task in the dressage ring, it never seems as daunting as repeatedly galloping at fences that I've been continually choking on.

Language barriers exist. My horse Wilson (aka "The Beastlet") is an absolute begging ham. While he enjoys being groomed and touched, nothing trumps anything edible.

Your Trainer Says:

"OK, LET'S TRY THAT *ONE MORE TIME...*"

Your Trainer Means:

YOU'RE GOING TO DO IT FROM

NOW UNTIL ETERNITY OR UNTIL YOU GET IT RIGHT.

Whichever comes first.

Love Languages and Horses

"Hmm, I'm sorry. I already gave you the rest of the cookies."

"You're a good boy though! You can have scritches for now. I'll see you tomorrow."

"Um, Excuse me? I need an offering, Peasant. I don't simply respond to touch and words of affirmation!"

That moment your horse *majikally* transforms into an OBSTINATE GIRAFFE...

Because sometimes 50 correction pads just don't cut it, but brand-new tack fixes everything. I used to think I just needed *one* saddle for myself; my horses have taught me otherwise.

Saddle Fitting Fun:

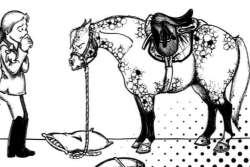

"Have you ever considered seeking professional help?"

Another exercise in futility…or a chance to practice some creative stretches or yoga moves. No matter how tall you are, or how short your horse is, he can become a giraffe. They can ALL BECOME GIRAFFES. I find this highly annoying; as usual, my horses are pleased with themselves.

Ah, yes, Newton, a classical instructor. For those who don't know, Newton's laws of motion are three physical laws that together laid the foundation for classical mechanics. They describe the relationship between a body and the forces acting upon it, and its motion in response to said forces. These seem like applicable concepts in the equestrian world.

"I thought you were into Natural Horsemanship?!"

"I am. I am using the **Natural Laws of Physics** right now!"

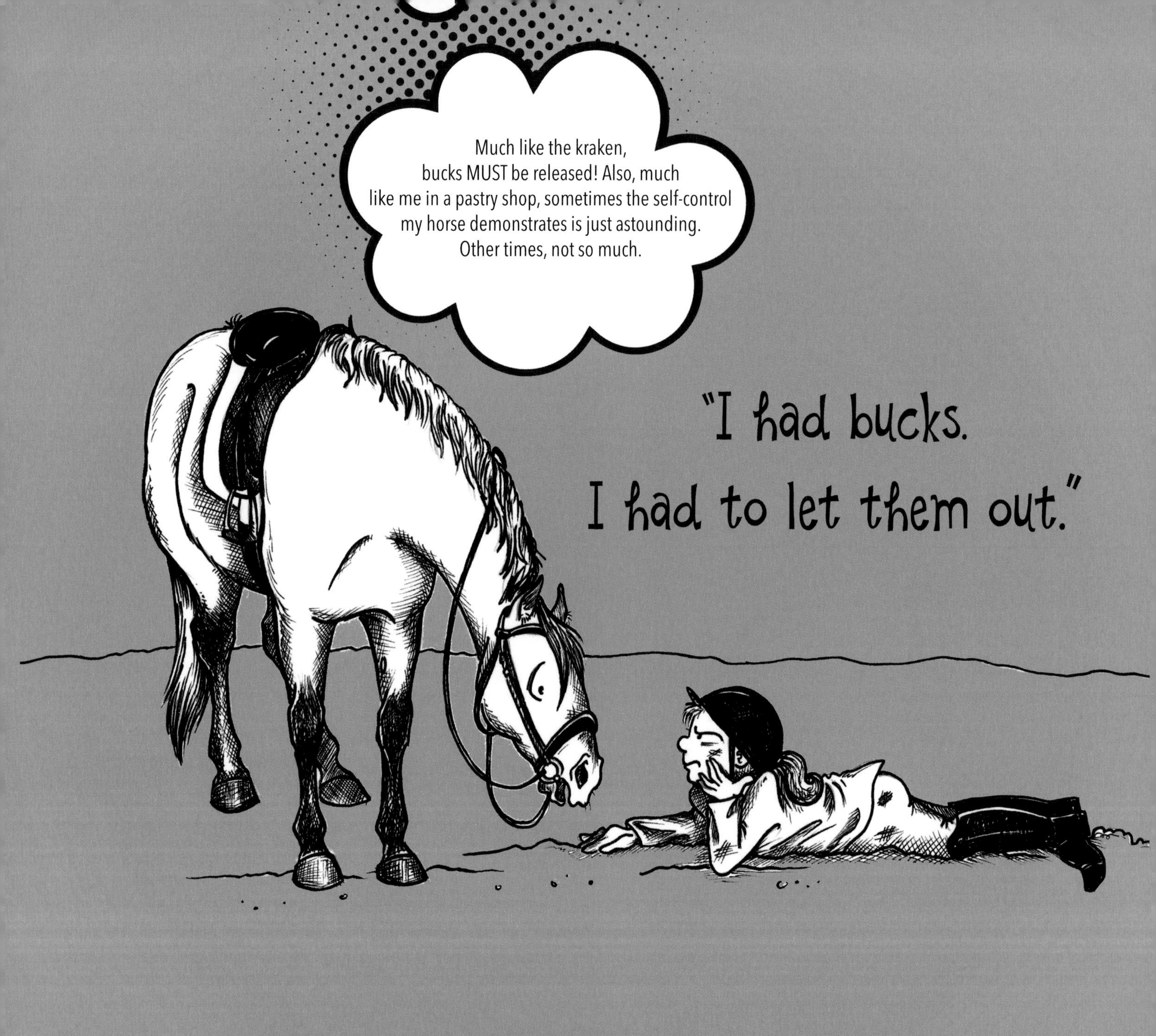
Much like the kraken, bucks MUST be released! Also, much like me in a pastry shop, sometimes the self-control my horse demonstrates is just astounding. Other times, not so much.
"I had bucks. I had to let them out."

Sad but True Equine Truth #22:

Just because you can buy the most expensive, talented, amazing horse out there, does NOT mean you can ride it.

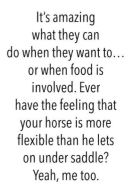

But even if you can't, hopefully you can at least dress him up nicely and go for the bling factor.

It's amazing what they can do when they want to… or when food is involved. Ever have the feeling that your horse is more flexible than he lets on under saddle? Yeah, me too.

Proprioception… IT'S A TRAP!

"But my body *IS* turned to the right!?"

As an instructor, I've often seen this fun play out, but just as much so, as a rider, I have experienced it. At first, I was incredulous when my instructor hinted that perhaps I was STILL. NOT. TURNING. I most certainly FELT like I was. I eventually realized the truth, and then the even bigger truth that things don't always feel as they are.

Equine Yoga:

Proof your horse can bend WHEN HE WANTS TO.

Indeed, we are pretty simple to train. Just ask any horse. Given that, this comic is dedicated to all of us who have been properly trained by our horses.

They're really pretty simple to train...

The extended trot is **NOT** just a more desperate medium trot.

Seriously. They're two different things. I promise. A friend of mine made this comment to our mutual coach and I thought that it was actually a pretty legitimate description of some trots I'd seen (and done) over the years. Of course, even if you can't always tell from watching, there really "should" be a difference....

Cantering is hard to do… especially when you're learning on a pony with an excellent extended trot. Anyone else have the joy of learning to canter on a nappy little pony beast who thinks trotting a million mph is a WAY better plan than actually cantering? Me neither, actually—I learned to canter on an ex-racehorse who liked to gallop off for funsies.

Learning to Canter:
IT'S HARD ON EVERYONE.

"Slide your leg back and…half-halt. He's running now. Bring him back… ask again…sit up…"

"Good try. Outside leg… other leg. Half-halt and outside leg again…"

"Hold on. Time for a pony motivator."

"Um, excuse me? I don't believe that she is qualified to have the stick.

Also, what's wrong with extended+ trot? The canter is overrated anyway."

WHACK!

"Fly."

WHACK!

"Fly."

WHACK!

"Fly."

"KNOCK IT OFF!
You know there is NO fly!"

"Fly"…"Annoying Small Predator"…. Same thing. File this under the category of things I "know" my horse is doing on purpose just to be passive-aggressively annoying (along with standing on the hose when I'm trying to bathe him and peeing on the new shavings right after I clean his stall). I'm fairly certain he does it to show his distaste for me ruining his afternoon nap, but I guess it could also be a statement on how he dislikes having his tail in a tail bag. Either way, he usually gets smacked back with it.

Story of my life…. My Warmblood ("The Beastlet") is quite content to schlep around doing stretchy work or walking on a long rein—even with the million heavy trucks, cars, and motorcycles that rampage along the miniature highway next to our ring. But pick him up and go to work and suddenly even the AIR is cause for spooking.

True Story…

"What's he spooking at?"

"The work."

Another Potential
Near-Death Equine Experience:

#Rudeness #WorseThanFalling #You'reNOTaLapDog #NoMoreTreatsForYou

"Hold still, Small Predator! It's still itchy where you made me wear the pully halter; I hates it!"

Rudeness…
I absolutely HATE being headbutted by a sweaty pony once the bridle is removed. None of my clients' horses do this nonsense. But then there's The Beastlet… he's a special kind of spoiled. It's a good thing I love him as much as I do or he'd be so dead.

Ahh, youth… baby Warmbloods…the closest thing you'll get to owning your own baby dragon. Get a young horse, they said…. It will be FUN, they said….

It was at that precise moment that Jane realized that perhaps today would NOT be the best day for young Diablo's first ride…

Optimum Operating Range for Young Horses:

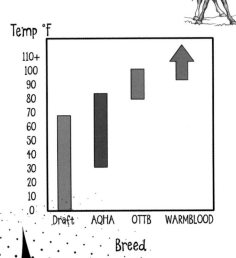

Temp °F

110+	
100	
90	
80	
70	
60	
50	
40	
30	
20	
10	
0	

Draft   AQHA   OTTB   WARMBLOOD

Breed

Optimum range in order to survive winter riding and to avoid getting launched into the stratosphere by your youngster this winter.

Poor life choices…they happen. We've all made them. Some of us just make them more frequently than others. (I am looking at you, Baby Horse.)

Poor Life Choices…

"You know you're not supposed to drop the Small Predators, right?"

The Disgruntled Lesson Horse:
ANOTHER REASON WE SHOULD BE THANKFUL THEY CAN'T TALK.

"Ok, seriously? Do you listen to anything that woman tells you?
You know you pay her an awful lot to run her mouth.

Did you hear her? It's INSIDE leg to OUTSIDE rein. It really isn't that difficult. I mean come on, I'm considered an appetizer on the food chain and even I get the concept. Geez.

And would you stop bouncing around? There's a reason she wants you to POST THE TROT: Because you CAN'T actually sit it!
I think you bruised my kidneys....

Are you seriously going to spur me again? Seriously?!
I'm beginning to think you should take up bowling or something."

I think we can all remember that saint of a horse who first sucked us into the horse world. Similarly, I think we can all also look fondly on the one who was a real snarkfest and taught us perhaps even more than we'd cared to know about how lucky we were that the aforementioned saintly horses exist.

Riding bareback.... Indicative of dedication or apathy? It's a toss-up, really. I'd like to pretend all my bareback riding has been because I'm tirelessly working on becoming awesome, but I'm afraid that's a bit of a stretch.

WHY OTHERS RIDE BAREBACK:

To further develop their seat, balance, and harmony with their horse.

WHY I RIDE BAREBACK:

I'm too lazy to tack up.

"Let's make a deal. You stay between my butt and the ground and you don't have to wear a saddle."

"You mean the torture girdle?"

Nobody loves this. Between the snow falling off the roof, wind against the back wall, and the demons that SURELY lurk in every dark corner, the indoor arena in the depths of winter is akin to some level of Dante's hell. Sometimes just surviving for 20 minutes counts as a win.

Winter Riding in the SCARY Indoor...

Because when you have to 'Work' for 45 minutes a day the #StruggleIsReal

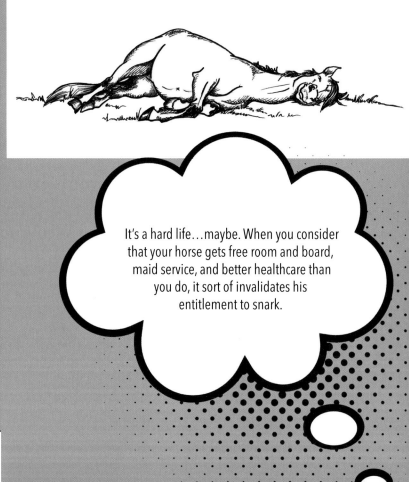

"WHAT?! I was GOOD! Nobody DIED! What do you people want from me?"

It's a hard life…maybe. When you consider that your horse gets free room and board, maid service, and better healthcare than you do, it sort of invalidates his entitlement to snark.

It never seems to work out this way, sadly. If the horse does it wonderfully, the temptation to get greedy and ask for another "one more time" is strong. If the horse is a stinker about it, then he gets to do it 100 more times so you don't end on a "bad note." It's perhaps best to remove that whole "one more time" phrase from your repertoire.

Yeah, he isn't wrong...

"Look, just do it ONE MORE TIME *NICELY* and you can be done!"

"This is a song of lies."

INTRODUCING THE UBER RARE
Shenanigansburger!

This breed has only recently been imported to the states from a super-secret island that only *I* know of! As such I am currently the only breeder of the Shenanigansburger in the U.S. Rest assured that my stock are superior in every way! Due to their ultra-rare status (note their super awesome brand and wild markings) these horses are a superior investment sure to make *you* money in the long run!

For a limited time, I have embryos from my top breeders starting at only $50K each. This is an amazing offer! **These horses have mind powers!**

If you want to be part of the next big thing, you'll have to act quickly as I am limiting my breeding this year to only 1000 foals!

Because we all want a horse that farts rainbows and butterflies, right? I know I sure do; it'd make cleaning stalls amazing.

Note the "kind eye" which clearly shows how loving and relaxed these guys are. they're obviously willing and searching for a majikal bond with their human..

The official brand denoting their royal heritage.

Awkward conformation that guarantees their inability to be competitive in any sort of *valid* discipline. This makes them unique and *speshul.* Others who own common breeds should be jealous.

Area responsible for rainbows and butterflies.

Unique coloring that guarantees that *everyone* who sees you will immediately know just how equine savvy you are.

Lots of extra hair that will make grooming an epic nightmare. however, it must *Never* be shorn as it gives the horse part of his *majikal* presence.

ON THE ROAD

(Showing as Spiritual Transcendence or
Nearing Bankruptcy with a Side of Nausea)

Ah, the joys of donning the oh-so-flattering white ensemble and dropping a couple grand to partake in a pressure-cooker type scenario for a $1.25 ribbon and a few panic attacks. We are a special crowd. As an added bonus, you get to be judged not only by the professional judges paid to do so, but also by every other living soul–rider or otherwise– who happens to amble by the ring while you're in. Sometimes, if you're really lucky, these individuals will also offer you some sage training advice. (Pro Tip: A case of wine is better than a bottle.) In addition to that whole "judgey" part of showing, your horse will undoubtedly present you with new and unique riding and training challenges.

CheckLists: Horse Show Edition

> Want to feel productive?
> Checklists! Now you can feel as accomplished as you'd like without actually being anything of the sort. My checklists do keep me organized, but there is a tendency to fluff them out with random, less significant tasks just so I can have the pleasure of checking them off and feeling more accomplished than I perhaps deserve to feel.

- ☑ Make list of stuff to accomplish
- ☑ Get health certificate
- ☑ Gas up truck
- ☐ Pay bills
- ☑ Think about what to load in trailer; make a list
- ☐ Actually load the trailer
- ☑ Eat stuff from around the house
- ☐ Do Laundry
- ☐ Pack clothes
- ☑ Text Michele back
- ☑ Pick nose
- ☑ Check email
- ☑ Check facebook
- ☐ finish comic before leaving."
- ☐ finish other random ungodly Sisyphean tasks . . .

How to feel instantly accomplished with the minimal amount of effort

Let the Games Begin...

"What are you doing?"

"Preparing for the show this weekend..."

> Horses are certainly…resourceful (much to our collective dismay). This is dedicated to all of you who have ever had your horse "inconveniently" require additional, last-minute farrier help.

An unfortunate trailering fact…
it's like the honeymoon suite for horses.
I don't know what "majikal" properties the trailer
has that can join two horses at the hip, but it's an
actual phenomenon. And god help you if one of
the horses in the trailer is a mare in heat.
You might as well just forget about ever
separating those two again.

HORSES:
Ride together in the trailer for 15 minutes….

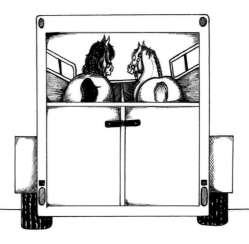

MARRIED FOR LIFE.

ANOTHER REASON SHOWING IS "FUN"...

The weather forecast the day you send your **non-refundable** show entry:

Mon	Tue	wed	Thu	Fri	Sat	Sun
SUNSHINE	SUNSHINE	SUNSHINE	SUNSHINE	SUNSHINE	SUNSHINE	SUNSHINE
72	74	77	71	75	77	74

The weather forecast the day after sending your **non-refundable** show entry:

Mon	Tue	wed	Thu	Fri	Sat	Sun
GARBAGE	TRASH	ABYSMAL	BULLS#*!	DITTO	SERIOUSLY?	FML
38	36	39	22	18	27	34

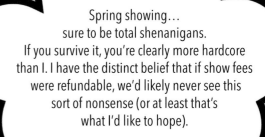

Spring showing…
sure to be total shenanigans.
If you survive it, you're clearly more hardcore
than I. I have the distinct belief that if show fees
were refundable, we'd likely never see this
sort of nonsense (or at least that's
what I'd like to hope).

Let's be honest…you're more spooky
(when it comes to noise) than your horse is.
That "fly hat" isn't just for the flies. In my case,
it's probably more for my mental benefit
than his. Oh, well, though.

"My mom is *sound sensitive.*"

"Why are you wearing a doily on your head?"

IF DRESSAGE LETTERS MADE SENSE:

WHAT YOU SEE VS WHAT YOUR HORSE SEES:
Dressage Show Edition

You: Dazzlingly clean, white show clothes.

Your Horse: New snot rags.

You: Trailer.

Your Horse: A carnival ride of doom.

You AND Your Horse:
THE JUDGEMENT BOX...

Can we vote to make this change?
Other possible letters include "FML" and "LMAO."
I cannot take credit for this idea,
but I can see it now: "OMG, extended bolt!"
"WTF, bulge shoulder out."

Let the show season begin!
Pretty sure the only thing more
frightening is the warm-up ring.

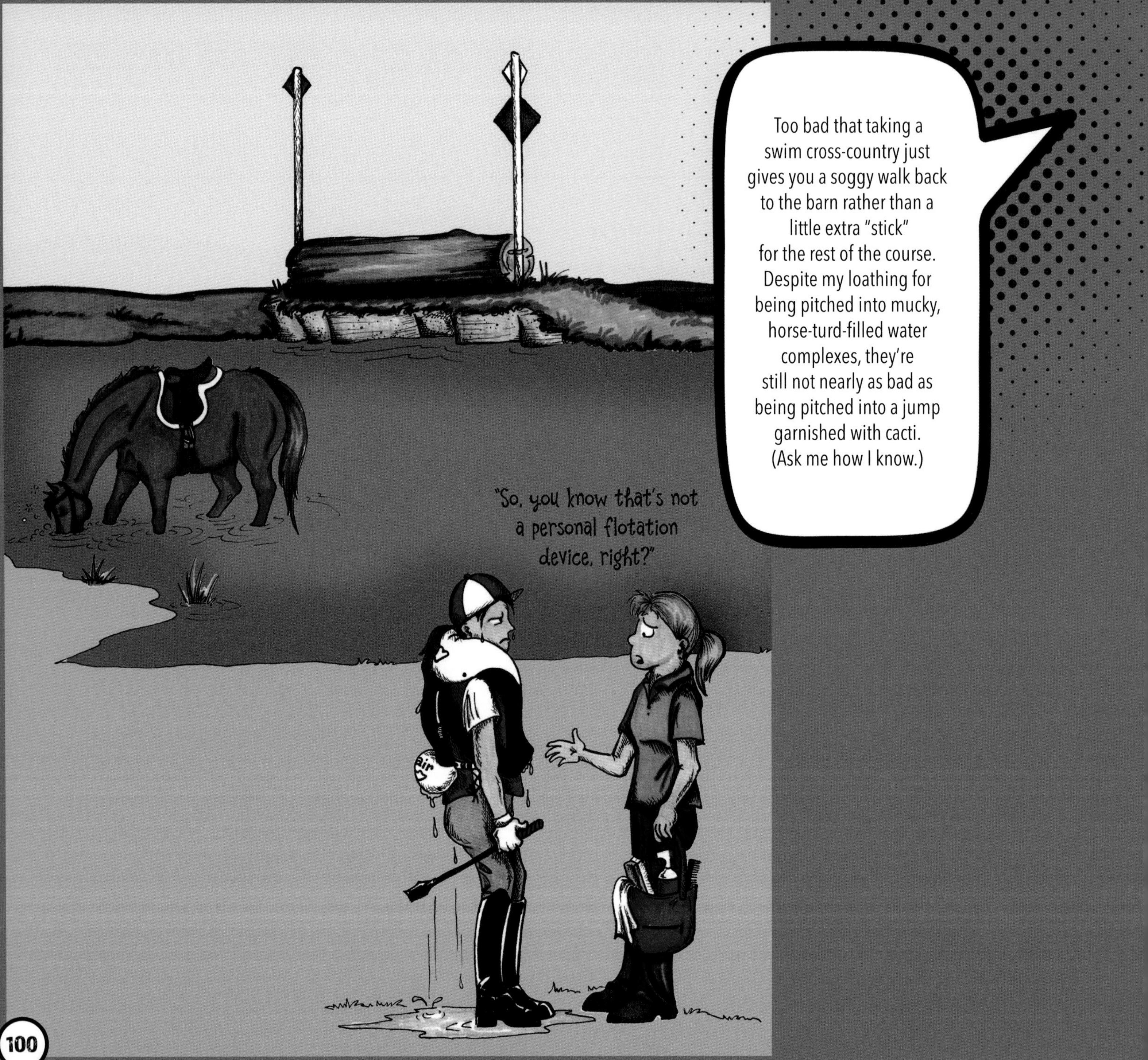
Too bad that taking a swim cross-country just gives you a soggy walk back to the barn rather than a little extra "stick" for the rest of the course. Despite my loathing for being pitched into mucky, horse-turd-filled water complexes, they're still not nearly as bad as being pitched into a jump garnished with cacti. (Ask me how I know.)
"So, you know that's not a personal flotation device, right?"

BRAIDING:
Another Exercise in Futility.

Excellent. Those aren't going anywhere.

These are leaving just as soon as you do.

It's always nice to return to the show grounds in the morning and find your horse has made many friends; everyone needs friends, after all. And to digest canvas strips. We all need that too.

Temporary Stalls = Perpetual Disaster

Braiding:
Another form of character building….
Have I mentioned that I'm not so much a fan of braiding? It's really too bad I'm OCD about it, since that forces me to do my own horses and most of my clients. No matter how many times I do it, I've yet to convince myself it's enjoyable–especially the next morning, when I'm fixing the braids that my equine darlings tried to rub out. Thankfully these days I do mostly dressage braids, which are much quicker and less arthritis-inducing than putting in 40-some hunter braids.

101

How I spend my time at a Horse Show:

GROOMING, MUCKING, AND TACK RESUSCITATING.

DOING ABSURD SHENANIGANS WITH MY FELLOW, EQUALLY DERANGED, HORSE SHOW FRIENDS.

TRAILERING

WAITING: TO SHOW, FOR FOOD, TO TACK UP, TO MEET FOR DINNER, TO BRAID, TO DIE FROM A HEAT STROKE... IT'S BASICALLY PURGATORY HERE.

Actually showing

Show time? More like time for shenanigans with others who are equally insane. Horse shows, despite their title as such, don't actually involve a great deal of "showing." At least not when compared to the amount of time spent doing everything else necessary to show at all.

Truth. Because being clad in ALL white is ALWAYS a flattering look. While I dislike heat stroke and the potential for head injuries from passing out while riding my horse, I also dislike looking like the Stay-Puft Marshmallow Man on a horse. I feel like we should have some in-between options for this.

"Did you hear? They waived jackets."

"Yes, but they've yet to waive vanity."

Lunging at the Horse Show:

"You look...QUIET.

You're lying. This is a trap."

"Soooooo relaxed. I love shows with crowds and dog-beast-predators and flappy tents of doom and heavy equipment and dumpsters and crackling sound systems...."

After Mounting:

"HaHaHa! KIDDING!"

Trying to keep your white horse white for a show...
THE DEFINITION OF FUTILITY.

"See? Doesn't that feel NICE?"

White horse problems...admittedly another variant on white girl problems. I have been acutely reminded of the pains involved in keeping the white or grey horse presentable. Despite 14 baths over a three-day period, and the fact that I think my fingers are permanently dyed purple, my horse still managed to find new and unique ways to make himself some shade of yellow, green, or brown.

Horses are LIARS. For real. Everything is a trap. I've grown very skeptical of my horse's AQHA lungeing routine.

SHOW NERVES:
#AllBeenHere

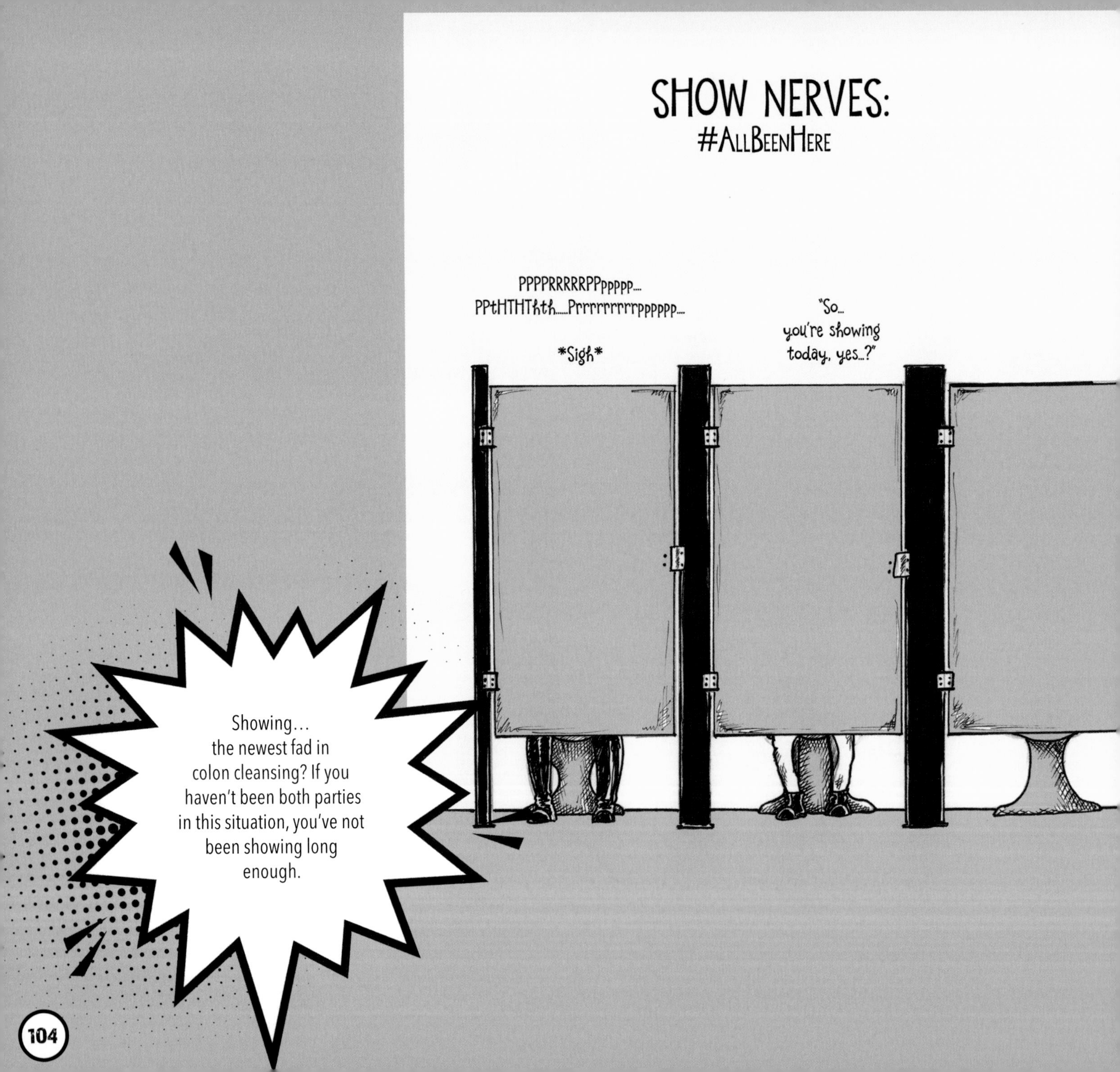
PPPPRRRRRPPppppp....
PPtHTHThth......Prrrrrrrrrpppppp....
Sigh
"So...
you're showing
today, yes...?"

Showing… the newest fad in colon cleansing? If you haven't been both parties in this situation, you've not been showing long enough.

Dressage Pit Crew

Pssssft...

Pssssft...

A similarity to Nascar...and on that note, if they can pay someone for making a bunch of left turns, I feel like they should be willing to pay someone for directing a 1,100-pound animal in a series of circles BOTH ways! This comic is for that 60 seconds before you go in the ring, when your horse is a lathered mess, he's still in his boots, you have mud all over your boots, and you're not quite sure where you laid your jacket.

I may be dating myself with this reference, but... "A" is also for "a$$hole." Horses who spook at things they're really not scared of fall into this category. Occasionally the letters K,E,H,C,M,B,F and a few others also bring about this reaction.

Today's Spook is Brought to You by...

The Letter 'A'
'A' is for Apple.

(What *other words* can you think of that start with the letter 'A'?...)

Show Clothes:
Just Another Exercise in Futility

8:15 AM

8:45 AM

While I really am grossly in love with the bling in the dressage ring, you have to admit that a little goes a long way.

If you've ever shown, you know I'm right on this one. Unless you have a herd of grooms and a hermetically sealed bubble to shroud yourself in, you'd better just face the fact that before you ever enter the ring, you'll be covered in a fine coating of horsey grunge.

If you can't Enchant them with Excellence...

Blind Them With Bling!

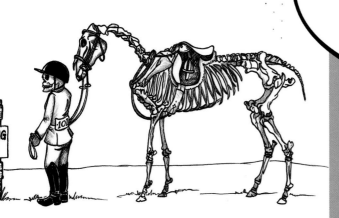

Hunter Shows...

Hunter shows be like...
NEVER-ENDING.
For all my hunter/jumper friends who know
the joys of waiting hours for your
class, only to finally go sit down and then
have it called so you can scramble
like mad to get ready again.
I don't miss that.

Show prep.
Because this is STILL
true.... Because
sometimes it's you who
needs to do 40 laps
before gracing the
warm-up ring.
Being a consummate
weenie myself, I can
attest to
this happening.

"First show.
She needs to lunge a little."

"Where are you going?
I thought you showed
this afternoon?"

WARNING:
CONTENTS UNDER PRESSURE

...9...8...7...6...5...4...3...

Time for some honest self-assessment: If you start off the cross-country phase trying to puke in such a manner so as to ensure the Gatorade coming out backward does not hit and spook your horse, all the while asking yourself what was so wrong with just doing plain old dressage, you might need to reconsider your riding goals. A moment similar to this may just have been when I realized that hurtling myself over fixed obstacles was not really my forte. Good thing I realized how wimpy I was early on, as it has given me plenty of time to throw my money and effort into an arguably even more expensive and somewhat masochistic discipline.
(Hello, Dressage.)

The Warm-Up Ring:
3 RING CIRCUS OR DANTE'S 7TH CIRCLE

WARM UP RING 2

How many horses can you fit into a 20- by 60-meter pen? It depends how high you stack them.

Though I recognize that the warm-up ring is a necessary evil at horse shows, I still don't understand why so many people riding in it are either feckless or believe they OWN the ring. Also, I get that there are green horses (I have one!), but let's all just agree not to take the screaming harpy on a string into the warm-up ring with 47 other horses when you have other options.

X. Halt. Salute! I'm pretty convinced that showing is in fact a form of masochism. If only we could all be as confident and competent going down center line as we are at nearly any other time when riding. Oh, well. Here's to dreaming (or at least some mild drinking before my next round of tests).

A. ENTER, WORKING TROT...   X. HALT. SALUTE.

Proceed with the realization that you've just forgotten EVERYTHING you THOUGHT you knew about how to ride dressage.

Dressage

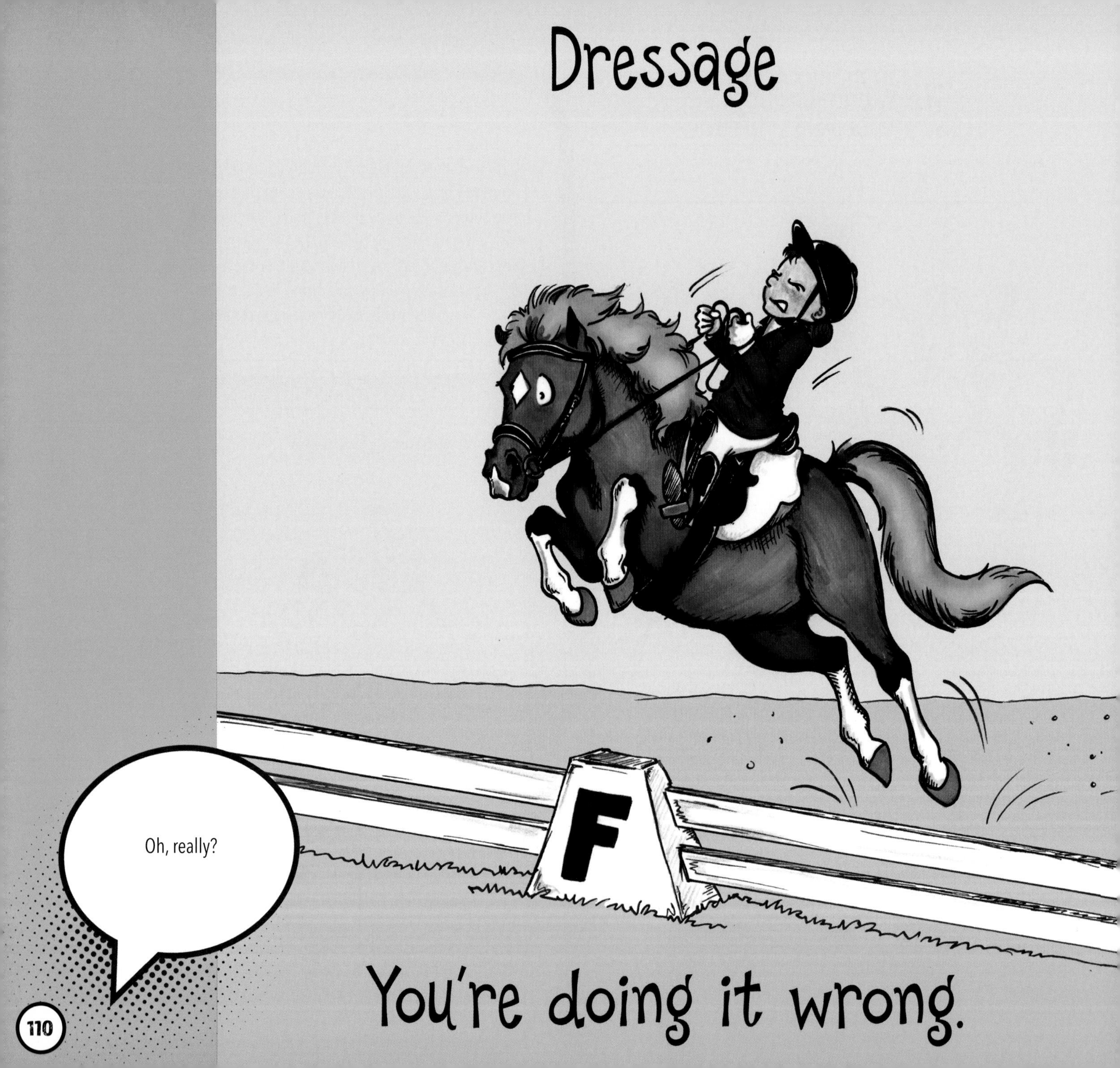

You're doing it wrong.

Oh, really?

Deciphering your test:
WHEN YOU WISH YOU HAD AN ADVANCED DEGREE IN GRAPHOLOGY

or maybe just some wine...

Sometimes there just isn't enough wine or patience.... I have a renewed amusement at the deciphering of the handwriting on dressage tests. To be fair, it is difficult to be a scribe, particularly at the upper levels where things happen quite quickly (so mad props and a thank you to all of you who even attempt to do this!). Nevertheless, there is certainly some humor to be taken from some of the stuff written (scrawled illegibly?) on tests.

2019 USEF FOURTH LEVEL TEST 2

PURPOSE
To confirm that the horse demonstrates correct basics, and has developed sufficient suppleness, impulsion and throughness to perform the Fourth Level tests which have a medium degree of difficulty. The horse remains reliably on the bit, showing a clear uphill balance and lightness as a result of improved engagement and collection. The movements are performed with greater straightness, energy and cadence than at Third Level.
READER PLEASE NOTE: Anything in parentheses should not be read.

INTRODUCE	ENTRY NO: 36
Counter change of hand in trot and canter; tempi changes every fourth stride; working partial pirouettes in canter	Conditions: ARENA SIZE: Standard AVERAGE RIDE TIME: 5:30 (from entry at A to final halt) Suggested to add at least 2 min. for scheduling purposes
Double Bridle Optional	MAXIMUM PTS: 380

		TEST	DIRECTIVES	POINTS	COEFFICIENT	TOTAL	REMARKS
1.	A X	Enter collected canter Halt, salute Proceed collected trot	Engagement, collection and quality of gaits; well defined transitions; straightness; attentiveness; immobility (min. 3 seconds)	7.0			☐ halt
2.	C M-B	Track right Shoulder-in right	Angle, bend and balance; engagement and collection	6.5			needs + △
3.	B-K K	Change rein, medium trot Collected trot	Moderate lengthening of frame and stride with engagement, elasticity, suspension, straightness and uphill balance; consistent tempo; well defined transitions	6.5			+ ↑ hill
4.	A D-E	Down centerline Half pass left	Alignment, bend, fluency and crossing of legs; engagement and collection	6.5	2	13	+ engage
5.	E-G C	Half pass right Track left	Supple change of bend; alignment, fluency and crossing of legs; engagement and collection	7.0	2		
6.	H-E	Shoulder-in left	Angle, bend and balance; engagement and collection	7.0			hotter △
7.	E-F F	Change rein, medium trot Collected trot	Moderate lengthening of frame and stride with engagement, elasticity, suspension, straightness and uphill balance; consistent tempo; well defined transitions	7.0			
8.	A K-R	Collected walk Change rein, extended walk	Regularity; suppleness of back; activity; overtrack; freedom of shoulder; stretching to the bit; well defined transitions	7.0	2	14	
9.	R M Between G & H	Collected walk Turn left Half pirouette left Proceed collected walk	Regularity; activity of hind legs; bend; fluency; size; self-carriage	5	2	10	too left
10.	Between G & M H	Half pirouette right Proceed collected walk Turn right	Regularity; activity of hind legs; bend; fluency; size; self-carriage	6.5	2	13	+ bat
11.		(Collected walk) [AK/RMG(H)G(M)GHC]	Regularity; suppleness of the back; activity; collection; self-carriage	7.0			
12.	C	Collected canter right lead	Precise, fluent transition; engagement and collection	6.5			rndr
13.	M-F F	Medium canter Collected canter	Moderate lengthening of frame and stride with engagement, elasticity, suspension, straightness and uphill balance; consistent tempo; well defined transitions	7.0			good
14.	A D-B	Down centerline Half pass right	Alignment and bend while moving fluently forward and sideways; engagement and collection	6.5			our bent
15.	B	Flying change of lead	Clear, balanced, fluent, straight flying change; engagement and collection	6.5			+ ↑↑
16.	B-G C	Half pass left Track left	Alignment and bend while moving fluently forward and sideways; engagement and collection	7.0			
17.	H-X Approaching X Toward M	On diagonal develop very collected canter Working pirouette left toward the letter M Proceed collected canter	Bend and balance of working pirouette; straightness, regularity, engagement and collection of canter	5	2	10 m → x + ⊘	

Could you please show me on this picture what letter of the alphabet that is?

I'm sorry, I can't even make that into a word.

Excuse me, could you please explain to me why you cross your 'L' like a 'T'?

These aren't letters...?

I'd like to buy a vowel, please.

Maybe you could draw me a diagram?

Why you should ALWAYS write the phonetic spelling of your horse's show name…
OR
how illiteracy claims innocent victims.

HORSE'S REGISTERED NAME:

Weltlady

(you know, by that lesser known Weltmeyer horse…)

WHAT THE ANNOUNCER SAYS:

"Next in the ring, **Wetlady**, ridden by someone now turning funny colors."

Remember that jump that you mocked during yesterday's course walk?

So does karma.

It's always the one you least expect…. I learned early in my short eventing career not to tempt the cross-country gods by belittling one of their own. Of course, the only fence I ever laughed at, I promptly ate the next day while on course. It would seem that humility is an important life lesson.

Packing the Trailer FOR a Show...

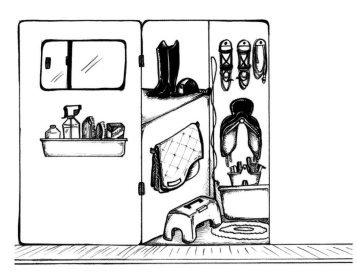

Packing the Trailer Heading Home FROM a Show...
AKA The Post Apocalyptic Packing

A sprained CNS....
This would explain my
short-lived eventing career.
I may actually suffer from this
debilitating injury
chronically.

The aftermath of a show…
or, how to turn your trailer into a black hole.
I can indeed attest to the shoddy packing job that
seems to happen when faced with the prospect of
FINALLY being done traveling.

The Most Dangerous Part of a Dressage Show:
THE AWARDS CEREMONY

'TIS THE SEASON

(Time to Spread Cheer...as in the Type That Goes with Adult Beverages)

Our horses are part of the family; it's only fair that they partake in the glory that is holiday cheer. Although I can't say any of my own beasts particularly love wearing antlers and taking selfies, they can be bought (or just forcibly coerced, if need be). This chapter looks at horse ownership through the holidays and how general harassment is a two-way street.

"Treat or Spook!"

"That's not how that goes."

"Don't be so sure of that. Do you really wanna risk it?"

Horses are all about spooks, tricks, and treats. I give my horses treats all the time and they regularly repay me with tricks.

Ah, Halloween…. Literally my very favorite holiday. Seriously. No joke here this time. (Given this particular exchange, I believe it would be in my best interest to acquiesce and go with the treat.)

"Treat or Trick, Kid. Your choice."

Horse Halloween Costumes:
THE DO-IT-THEMSELVES-EDITION

'DIRT'
This is a year-round favorite, though it is especially popular in the Spring and whenever you're short on time and want to ride.

'ALMOST-HEADLESS-HORSE'
Synonymous with the equine superhero, **"El Destructo."**
This is a particular favorite among the younger Warmblood crowd.

'ZOMBIE APOCALYPSE'
Also known as, "Hey-Did-You-Know-Your-fence-is-Down?" and "Never-Ending-Vet-Bills." for many horses, this one never seems to get old.

Because everyone likes to play dress up…. This situation is probably akin to why responsible parents don't let their toddlers dress themselves.

It's scary because it's true. Ah, what could be more frightening than reality?

So many unanswered questions…
like where did all those pumpkins
come from? And whose laundry
did Woody steal? Are those fishnets?

Things I am Thankful for as an Equestrian:

DUCT TAPE AND BAILING TWINE
With these two items you could quite possibly conquer the world.

DIVINE INTERVENTION
No matter what your belief on the afterworld, there are some days you're pretty stoked you've managed not to pay it a visit.

FAMILY
Who else is there to listen to you (even when you're full of it), comfort you (even if you've done something foolish), laugh with you (and sometimes AT you), and put up with your shenanigans?

"I know they're family, but next year I think you need to cook dinner."

"And we are especially thankful today for this beautifully prepared feast of gloriousness for which I have totally outdone myself..."

> Things to be thankful for usually include me not cooking. I'm also thankful for things like coffee and Advil.

Thanksgiving is Over:
YOU'RE OFFICIALLY FREE TO TORTURE EVERYONE WITH CHRISTMAS NOW...

"Don't worry, I'll discuss this little transgression with her in the clinic this weekend...."

> If you're like me, you are ready to get the tree and 87,000 lights up and going after dinner on Thanksgiving. Now anything Christmas is fair game—even harassing your animals with those fun-filled holiday photo shoots.

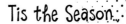

Tis the Season...

to cause much disgruntlement for your pets.

Every pony deserves a hat and some antlers. 'Tis the season to fully irritate your pets and be thankful that they don't have the opposable thumbs to retaliate (of course, they do have other ways).

"I know someone who is getting lumps of PONY COAL and a trip to play in the arena footing for Christmas."

I'm fairly certain that unless you're up on what a "eunuch" is, this will make absolutely no sense. I'm sorry.

"They're actually pretty good, but why are their voices so high?"

"Well, they ARE geldings..."

Lumps of "pony coal"? I think I'd rather have "real coal," actually. I'm fairly certain if Santa were to poll my horses, they would all agree that I've been particularly naughty this year (what with all that riding and training business, muzzles, spurs, and depriving them of the copious amounts of food they believe they deserve). Guess it's a good thing they don't get to voice their opinions.

"First of all, this is demeaning and totally unacceptable! Also, SANTA brought you a GIFT..."

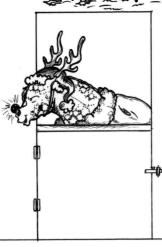

"...it's floating in my automatic waterer."

Another reason your horse bucks you off...

"You will regret this. Maybe not today, maybe not tomorrow, but soon...."

Can't say I blame them for their clear disdain over this sort of thing.

The Joy of the Season...
Is Often Edible.

"Small Predator!
You are here! I am so glad.
You are my VERY FAVORITE STAFF!
I see you come bearing JOY."

"Your sincerity is questionable."

Find your joy…just not too much, if you wanna fit into your breeches in January. The season of cookies, cakes, candies, and pies is here! Oh, yeah, and peace, love, and happiness… those too.

Because NO ONE Likes the Creepy Elf… Seriously. Have you ever even looked at it? In what world is it NOT terrifying to convince your kid that a small, creepy-looking elf is lurking in the house and that he comes ALIVE at night to spy on you all and report back to his master?

"Have you seen Taylor's
Elf on the Shelf?
She thinks maybe she left it here."

"Haven't seen the creepy elf.
I could introduce you to the
Connoisseur of Manure though…"

A Pony's Christmas List:

Dear Sandy Claws (Most revered of the small, two-legged predators),

I'm writing to you with my wish list! I'VE BEEN PARTICULARLY GOOD THIS YEAR, only having dumped my mom once--maybe twice--a month or so ago when she was being particularly annoying. She and I are cool though. Promise.

1. Horse treats—as in all of them. I want all the treats. That should last me a week or so.
2. A new wearable tug-of-war tarp. My current one is pretty used up, especially after my pasture mate and I managed to remove it and bury it in the frozen mud (mom wasn't very impressed; sometimes she's boring like that).
3. A few more small predator servants. I know I have quite a few now that cater to my every need but it couldn't hurt to have a few extra. I especially need a new farrier servant since I think I've worn out my other one (oops). I do NOT need another trainer predator; those are annoying and tiresome to deal with. In fact, if you could take back my current one that'd be great.
4. More mud holes; they're great for spa treatments and hiding all the worthless things mom likes to make me wear.
5. My own opposable thumbs would be swell. Then I wouldn't need to rely on my servants as much. It's a win/win.
6. A giant sugar lick. I don't like those salty ones very well.
7. Did I already mention treats? Lots of them.
8. A new rubber feeder Frisbee. Mine somehow has big holes in it now...
9. More of that cold white stuff; it seems I have to do WAY less trotting around in circles when that stuff is around.
10. Pockets on mom's jacket for me to stick my nose in. Preferably full of treats.

I think that's all for this year, Sandy!

Love,
Woody

"Dare I look?"

I can only imagine the sorts of absurdity that would arise from my beasts writing to Santa.

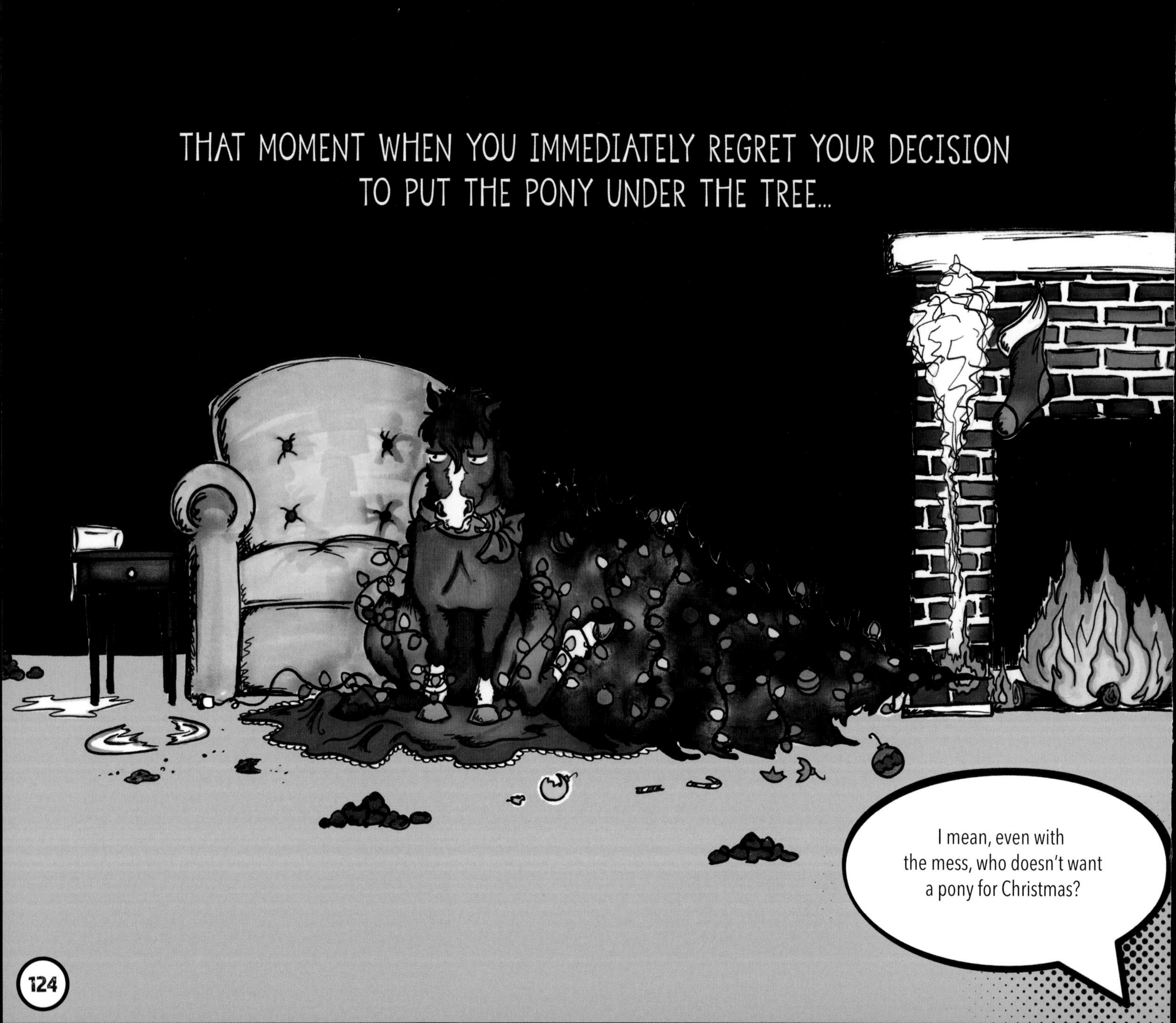
THAT MOMENT WHEN YOU IMMEDIATELY REGRET YOUR DECISION TO PUT THE PONY UNDER THE TREE...
I mean, even with the mess, who doesn't want a pony for Christmas?

NEW YEAR'S RESOLUTIONS
that I WOULD have Made if I Thought I Could Actually Keep Them:

1. I will spend at least 10% of my time in a relatively sanitary state, sans hay and shavings in my hair and my being lacking its usual film of dust and horse excrement.

2. I will make a concerted effort to buy clothes that are appropriate to wear among the general populace instead of blowing all my money on stretchy pants with funny little bits of erratically placed leather.

3. I will get home from the barn before 7:00 p.m.

4. I will spend daily quality time with The Fiancé that doesn't include the 15 minutes before I pass out on the couch.

Sadly, I've never been so hot at keeping up with any sort of New Year's Resolutions. If I were, then I'd be 15 pounds lighter, running marathons, finishing my doctorate, and wildly famous.

5. I will never again take on a "free" horse.

BOTTOMLESS PIT
* SHOVEL MONEY * HERE

6. I will also stop perusing Craigslist, Dream Horse, equine.com, etc "just to look."

7. I will take The Fiancé's credit card information off of my SmartPak account.

It's time for that whole painful process of getting your life back on track. I know I'm more concerned with being prepared for show season than a day on the beach (even as a Floridian, I've never been too keen on frolicking in ankle-deep murk, wondering what critters are touching me).

IF NEW YEAR'S RESOLUTIONS WERE FORCED:

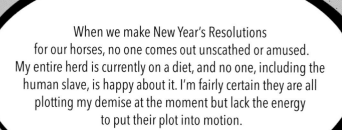

"This is an outrage! I am pretty sure no one locked you in a cell and forced you to survive by eating salad through a colander when those white breeches of yours started looking a little lumpy!"

MICRO-GRAZE

JANUARY 1ST:

Normal women vow to get fit for bathing suit season.

Dressage queens vow to get fit because no bathing suit in the world is as revealing as white show breeches.

"I told you that fudge was a bad idea. I was just looking out for you."

When we make New Year's Resolutions for our horses, no one comes out unscathed or amused. My entire herd is currently on a diet, and no one, including the human slave, is happy about it. I'm fairly certain they are all plotting my demise at the moment but lack the energy to put their plot into motion.

If Horses Made New Year's Resolutions

"I will only spook at TRULY TERRIFYING things (like plastic bags, butterflies, and my own poo when it's cold outside and it steams)."

"I'm pretty sure my guys also resolve to find even more new and exciting ways to maim themselves and subsequently drive me crazy."

"I will wait at least a week before 'LOSING' my new shoes somewhere in turnout."

"I will eat horse cookies only in MODERATION."

"I will wait AT LEAST FIVE MINUTES before peeing in my new shavings."

"I will be SENSITIVE to my rider's LIGHTEST aids."

"I will refrain from destroying MY OWN blanket."

"I will make sure my human knows how much I love her (And her magic, treat producing pockets...)."

Top 10 Equestrian
New Year's Resolutions...

That will never happen.

10. I will clean out the dust, grain, manure, and miscellaneous tack from my car monthly or before I subject any non-horsey friends to it.

9. I will get home from the barn in a *timely manner. *

8. I will not spend hours mindlessly searching Facebook tack trading sites for tack I don't actually need but MUST get because it's a 'good' deal.

7. I will not spoil my horses.

6. I will feed The Husband before the horses (on most nights).

5. I won't do my horse laundry in the house washing machine.

4. I will clean my tack *well* after every ride.

3. I will clean the house and bathroom before the barn.

2. I will use my discretionary income for things other than the horses.

1. I will not buy another horse this year.

"It's ok,
she loves you too,
Small Grumpy Predator.
Do you need a cookie?"

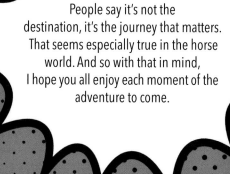

People say it's not the destination, it's the journey that matters. That seems especially true in the horse world. And so with that in mind, I hope you all enjoy each moment of the adventure to come.

Valentine's Date Night
Tip #12:

No matter how cute he says you look in your breeches and boots and no matter how UNNATURAL it is for you, you SHOULD be sure to leave enough time to shower and change into NORMAL PEOPLE clothes before going out. Trust me, your date & everyone within 20 meters will appreciate it.

Just a heads up…
that is, of course, unless you enjoy making others bask in the aroma of hay and horse manure. It's not my place to judge. You should also probably plan to be home from the barn before dark that night too. (Pro Tip: I find that The Fiancé gets grumpy if I'm more than three hours late for dinner plans.)

The truth can be awkward….
But when aren't relationships awkward? Valentine's Day is over-hyped. But, even if you're single with regards to another human counterpart, you always have your four-legged beasts. And let's be honest, no one adores you more than your horse when you're holding a cookie.

"Hello, Favorite Human!
What GLORIOUS Valentine offering have you brought me?
We all know that you love ME most."

RELATIONSHIP GOALS:
WHEN YOUR NON-HORSEY SIGNIFICANT OTHER *REALLY* KNOWS YOU...

"Wow! How did you know I need more tack?!"

Not that horse people are ever "difficult" to decipher... (Because our other equestrian friends don't enable us enough.)

VALENTINE'S DAY POETRY FROM A PONY...

"Roses are red,
All I do is make poo.
Give that a try,
And see if she still loves you."

Mom,

Thank you
FOR PUTTING UP WITH ALL OF MY ANTICS!

It's amazing that more mothers don't eat their own young. There's a reason some of us should never spawn; mine is that I know how I was as a small child. Between my horse-crazy sisters and I and the ever-growing menagerie, it's a good thing my mother was gifted with more patience than any reasonable person should have. So, here's to you, moms! Thanks for not selling us on the black market!

Dear, Dad...

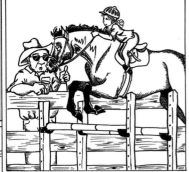

Thanks for always knowing what to do with that ornery horse...or at least convincing us that you did.

And for always being there, even after I sent you away while I was puking in the start box.

And for taking to the sidelines, giving up every free moment of your life, & every spare dollar, to support a house full of girls & their horse addiction.

And for making us all learn the joy of horses & showing even if it was against our will & involved moving to the boonies.

But most of all, Dad, thank you for giving so much of yourself to your family & making life with horses possible. We will never forget those weekends spent showing together as a family. (even if at the time we may have been plotting each other's demise).

Happy Father's Day, Dad.

We love and miss you.

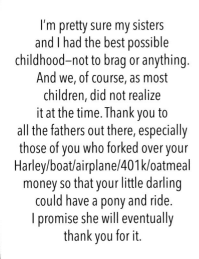

I'm pretty sure my sisters and I had the best possible childhood—not to brag or anything. And we, of course, as most children, did not realize it at the time. Thank you to all the fathers out there, especially those of you who forked over your Harley/boat/airplane/401k/oatmeal money so that your little darling could have a pony and ride. I promise she will eventually thank you for it.

IF HORSES ARE FROM HEAVEN

(Then Ponies Are from Hell...
and Mares Are the Overlords of Hell)

We love our horses. If we didn't, there really would be no reason to partake in the never-ending shenanigans they provide. We would also all probably have second homes on Mustique, or maybe a private jet—but I digress. Even though we love our beasts, it's likely a fair assessment to say that some are more challenging than others: I'm looking at you, ponies and mares. But since when do equestrians shy away from a challenge?
(Pro Tip: All things are possible with the blood of Christ—i.e. red wine.)

This may explain why parents get their kids ponies…of course, there is the possibility that they actually do, in fact, hate their children. Ah, ponies. So obscenely adorable, so incredibly naughty. As evil as they can be, it's hard not to love them just the same—although I imagine it's a little easier for those who've never been had by one to love them.

Ponies:

What the Uninitiated See:

"Aww! How cute! I'll ride that one because it's little and SAFE!"

What The Rest of Us See:

"No way! Anything under 14.3 is THE DEVIL!"

Wait for it…ponies are sticklers for technique. The only way to handle a situation like this is to brush yourself off and vow to return with tools for round two.

Ah yes, the Mare Glare.
Truly an all-purpose expression.
I feel the need to once again state that I love a good mare. Since I make a very similar face when approached by most everyone, I guess perhaps I can relate to mares with regards to this.

Mares…

"Hey, remember when you used the whip a little too hard last Tuesday?"

"Yeah, me too. We're even now."

So before you go hating on me for this, let me just say that some of the VERY best horses I've ever had have been mares and I do believe that a good mare will give you 110%. That being said, they also tend to have a wicked sense of "justice" and will be the first to let you know if you're riding like an idiot (or sometimes just that they *think* you are).

Don't let him fool you…

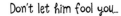

'PONY' is a FOUR LETTER WORD.

I believe that ponies are the equine equivalent of used car salesmen: you think you're getting the deal of a lifetime until you get home and then you realize you've mostly been taken for a ride (usually through a manure-filled back pasture and over a few barbed wire fences along the way).

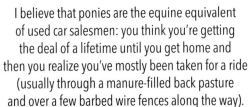

Ask Icee:

Dear Icee,
My human keeps sticking me with her spurs. What should I do?

-Stuck in NV

Dear Abby,
meet Icee. Really, with some horses, I'm more than glad they can't talk.

Dear Stuck,

How horrid. That sort of behavior isn't to be tolerated. The first thing to do is assess how willful your rider is; the last thing you want is to pick a fight you can't win. With the majority of riders, my standard M.O. is generally to start small; **you don't wanna go all War Horse and cause your owner to get that trainer person involved-- those are much harder to work with.**

That being said, my favorite first tactic is the pin and spin. As soon as you feel the spur immediately pin your ears and snake your head around angrily. Timing is everything. If done properly, this exercise will allow your rider to connect your agitation to the spur. Be patient though, as it is a learning experience and some riders are slower than others to catch on.

Usually, this move is enough to deter most novice riders. If I have a particularly stubborn one, I will escalate to kicking out both back feet and then refusing to move. That generally does the trick and as a bonus gets you out of work too.

Remember, you want your rider to learn the subtleties of your cues. This is another reason to start small and gradually increase your aids. With patience and persistence you'll be able to flick an ear back and have her remove her spurs. Really, it can be done.

THIS IS THE WRONG APPROACH

REMEMBER, ALL HUMANS CAN BE TAUGHT.

Best of luck to you.
~Icee

PRACTICE THIS INSTEAD

Icee is a 13 year old Swedish Warmblood mare. Her interests include eating, sleeping, and lolling in the pasture. When she's not enjoying her 23 hours a day of 'personal time,' she's working diligently to ensure that her human knows just how woefully inadequate her riding skills are. Icee is a staunch supporter of equine rights and is a proud member of both L.A.M.E.E (League of Assertive Mares for Equine Equality) and S.Q.U.E.A.L. (Society of Queens United for Equine Advancement and Livelihood).

There are Some Days When You Need to Think like a Pony:

AKA: ASSESS THE SITUATION AND POLITELY DECLINE

"I'm sorry, but I'm done participating in this activity today."

Once, while driving, my friend simply declared, "I'm done participating in today." Not really knowing what to say (or what that meant, because how does one stop participating in a day?) my mind ran wild with images of throwing oneself from the moving vehicle, willing oneself to simply drop dead, and a few other relatively awkward scenarios–I just sort of burst out laughing. Obviously, despite the impossibility of it (barring any dire actions anyway), there are just some days that I think we'd all like to simply "'stop participating in." Sadly, as that's not usually an option, I generally find that I myself end up resorting to petulant sulking with the occasional stream of obscenities.

MY PONY'S FACE WHEN HE'S INFORMED IT'S DIET TIME.

The Face of Disgust....
If looks could kill, I'd be dead
100 times over, for sure.

"Today I shall behave myself.
No silly spooking over nothing."

"TINY TOXIC DRAGON BUG!"

They say it takes
us 21 days to build a new habit.
Given how hard it is for me to form
good habits, I'd say they're correct (gym
every morning? *Pfttt*. Right). I'd also say
my horse has equal difficulty learning new
good habits. The same cannot be said,
however, for naughty ones; he is quite
quick to pick those up.

"Sorry.
I forgot myself there
for a moment."

Ask Icee:

Dear Icee,
My human insists on riding me daily,
sometimes for an HOUR at a time. I think
this is a bit excessive but she doesn't
seem to acknowledge my protests. What
should I do?

-Ridden Hard and Put Away Wet

"Ask Icee," take two...
because we all actually care about her
thoughts and opinions on things. (Why,
yes, I do think horses are smart enough
to come up with this sort of ploy.)

Dear Ridden,

That is indeed unacceptable. Just because your owner supplies you with room service, maid service, and 23 hours to do with as you please, doesn't make it okay for her to foist manual labor upon you on a daily basis. Repeat this to yourself: This is NOT okay. OWN IT. BELIEVE IT. Now let's do something about it.

In this type of situation there are a few different approaches you can try. The first is to make your irritation more obvious. I suggest ear pinning, head shaking, or the occasional kicking out at the leg. Just be sure to keep your reactions on the cusp of what your rider can handle. If you go all Chuck Norris on her she may freak out and send you to the trainer, which will NOT result in less work.

If acting out forcefully isn't something you're comfortable with, you can try the more Zen approach of doing nothing. Yes, absolutely nothing. Do not be baited by your rider. Refuse to move no matter what she does. BE A LUMP; A BIG, 1400LB, HAIRY, IMMOBILE, LUMP. Honestly, what can she do? Have you ever seen a 120lb human heave a horse any sort of distance? I DIDN'T THINK SO.

Another possible approach, and my personal favorite, is to feign lameness. To really sell it though, it helps if you can actually slightly maim yourself. Nothing serious mind you, you don't want to be stuck on stall rest forever. I recommend sticking your foot through the fencing (or giving it a good kick) --doing so usually results in some surface abrasions and a bit of swelling which are great for eliciting sympathy. Once this is done, do your best to hobble about—Do NOT, under any circumstances, let your rider see you trotting or cantering around or the jig will be up. When your rider tries to feel your leg, be sure to jerk it away and look pathetic. If she tries to hose it, lift it way up high and look pathetic. If she goes to hand walk you, drag your leg and look pathetic. If you play this right, you can get out of quite a bit of work all the while avoiding that whole nasty stall rest business.

The added benefit of pretending to be lame is that you can drag it out for quite some time. In fact, if you work it, you could easily drag out the whole ordeal for months at a time by continuing to be 'mildly off'--you can also change the leg you're lame on to really confuse things. Just be sure that if a vet is called to perform a lameness exam that you trot off perfectly sound. That will ensure that the exam is brief and that they don't do much which will allow you to resume your little ruse at a later time and your rider will most likely assume the vet just wasn't thorough enough.

Hopefully I've given you some ideas on how to start a positive dialogue with your rider so that the appropriate changes will be made. Be persistent and you'll get your way.

Best of luck to you.
~Icee

Icee is a 13 year old Swedish Warmblood mare. Her interests include eating, sleeping, and lolling in the pasture. When she's not enjoying her 23 hours a day of 'personal time,' she's working diligently to ensure that her human knows just how woefully inadequate her riding skills are. Icee is a staunch supporter of equine rights and is a proud member of both L.A.M.E.E (League of Assertive Mares for Equine Equality) and S.Q.U.E.A.L (Society of Queens United for Equine Advancement and Livelihood).

Life with a Mare:

Mares... so many opinions, so little time.

LYRIC: "Being ridden is dumb.
The gate is over there you know.
You could, you know, LEAVE.
Hey, look...a mounting block.
I bet it also works as a DISMOUNTING
block too. You should try it."

ALSO LYRIC: "What do you MEAN I have the day off?
Being ridden is my JOB. It's what I DO and I do it EVERY DAY.
Walk your stumpy little legs into that tack room right now
and get your helmet so we can go!
What kind of slapdash dog and pony show do you think you're running here?
IDIOT."

A Gift Horse...

Stay away from his mouth.
(And probably his hind end too for good measure.)

Gift horses—guaranteed to bite you in the....
Though my illustration doesn't accurately depict
what the original saying really means (which is that
one should be appreciative), I do feel that if you're
gifted a small, hairy beast, it is indeed sound advice
to stay away from the business ends, as there's
probably a reason he was a "gift."

141

That moment when you begin to suspect that your pony's SENSITIVITY under saddle is nothing more than a clever ruse.

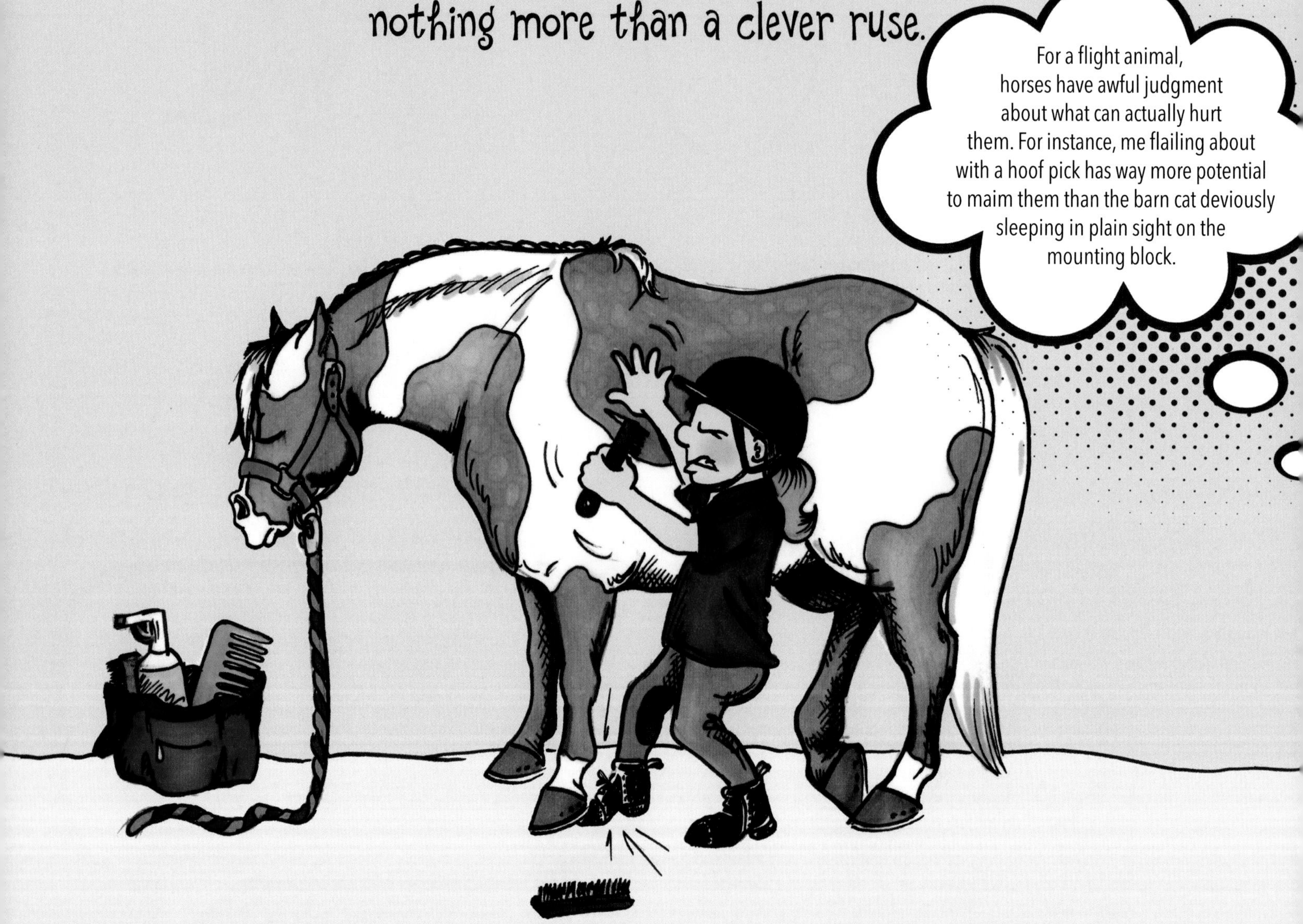
For a flight animal, horses have awful judgment about what can actually hurt them. For instance, me flailing about with a hoof pick has way more potential to maim them than the barn cat deviously sleeping in plain sight on the mounting block.

Ask Icee:

Dear Icee,

My rider has decided to take up jumping. I am a dressage horse. Yes, I have been trained in jumping, but I am staunchly against it. Horses are not meant to be leaping through the air! I have tried both gentle refusing and then just plain STOPPING as well as going around the jump, but nothing has worked! Sometimes I fear that my rider may be a bit... uh, slow. All my attempts have caused her to do is use SPURS, and a CROP. I need your help, Icee! This is a serious violation of my rights as an Equine! Please help.

—Not Jumping Through Hoops

Dear Hoops,

You're right that your rights have been egregiously trod upon; how dare your rider ask you to do something you've been trained for and thus already know you dislike! Nevertheless, you've gone about voicing your concerns to your rider in entirely the wrong way (anything that causes a rider to get spurs and a whip is always counterproductive for you). If you don't want to be a jumper, then all you have to do is jump, and by jump I mean **hurtle your fuzzy butt over things like you've been flung by a** trebuchet.

This may seem counterintuitive, but humans are an odd species and when it comes to training a horse to jump they will go to no end to train a horse who refuses to jump (don't ask me why, it's probably because humans are in fact a somewhat slow, hard-headed species). However, a horse that willingly jumps but is just terrible at it will generally be relegated to the dressage ring or as a trail horse with little more than a sigh and shrug of the shoulders. Keeping this in mind, it is clear that all you have to do to avoid being asked to jump is to jump so badly that your rider fears for her life (**go ahead, channel your inner deer; maybe even one with its** derriere on fire). Note though that this does not mean that you misbehave as all that will do is get you thrown into full training (and we all know my thoughts on the nuisance that trainers are). Instead, you must always appear to be a willing participant, albeit an untalented one.

JUST AN EXAMPLE, PLEASE DO NOT SET FIRE TO SMALL WOODLAND CREATURES

I recommend that you keep your rider guessing. One moment be entirely too forward, then go into sloth mode. Occasionally leap straight up over the fence, retract your legs, and land on it. Go long, chip in, **but never, ever find a spot.** Sometimes it's also fun to crash through it without even attempting to lift your feet up. You get the gist of it. Have fun with it, but never give your rider any hope that you might have even one ounce of talent or she may persist even longer with her pipe dream of making you a jumper.

Remember, the more awkwardly you can soar through the air, flailing your legs in every which way, the better chance you'll have that you're rider will stop asking for this sort of activity. In fact, if you play this right you should be done with this silly jumping thing by the end of the week (maybe by next week if your owner is a bit more masochistic than most riders).

Best of luck,
~Icee

Icee is a 13 year old Swedish Warmblood mare. Her interests include eating, sleeping, and lolling in the pasture. When she's not enjoying her 23 hours a day of 'personal time,' she's working diligently to ensure that her human knows just how woefully inadequate her riding skills are. Icee is a staunch supporter of equine rights and is a proud member of both L.A.M.E.E (League of Assertive Mares for Equine Equality) and S.Q.U.E.A.L (Society of Queens United for Equine Advancement and Livelihood).

More sound advice from Ms. Sunshine-and-Light herself, Icee. (I think my last Thoroughbred went this route...)

Ask Icee:

Dear Icee,

My human wants to start 'showing dressage.' I'm not sure what that is but *I AM sure I want nothing to do with the mobile bear cave on wheels* that she wants to put me in. It was a close call yesterday and I don't know if I will escape next time. What should I do to let my human know I want nothing to do with this?

–Not Bear Bait

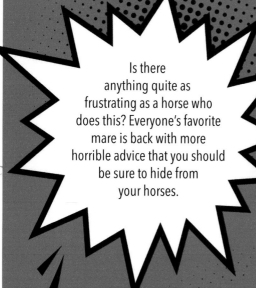

Is there anything quite as frustrating as a horse who does this? Everyone's favorite mare is back with more horrible advice that you should be sure to hide from your horses.

Dear Bait,

You're right to avoid the mobile bear cave; *many a horse has entered never to return!* My personal experience with these, in my younger, more vulnerable years, is that they generally transport you to a boot camp of sorts where your rations will be significantly decreased, your work load will be through the roof, and your housing situation will be reduced to standing in a flapping tent that, given its overall shoddiness, I can only assume was rigged together by carnies. This is not a pleasant place to be I assure you.

The trick to avoiding this Hell on Wheels is actually much easier than you'd think; you must simply stand quietly and refuse to budge. Now I know that this seems counterintuitive, given that whole flight instinct, but it's the only way. The problem with jumping about, running circles, or trying to bolt is that humans are clever enough to use any momentum you provide against you. You leap up in the air; they'll pull you forward. You bolt; they'll use a chute and run you in. The fact of the matter is that if you sit like a large, hairy lump your human is left with very few options. This is ALWAYS a good thing for you.

To start, when you're led to the cave stop short of it and stare it down. Your human will be reluctant to try to physically harass you, thinking instead that maybe you're scared (you can further this little ruse by snorting some and showing the whites of your eyes). Your human will most likely try to lure you in with goodies. You can play this to your advantage. Offer a step closer to the bear cave; get a cookie. Snort, get wide-eyed, shake a little, and take a small step back. Your human will reassure you. Continue this game until you have eaten all the cookies your human has to offer. NEVER get within 2 feet of the cave.

Eventually your human will catch on to this game (some are sharper than others so this will vary). At this point most humans will get frustrated, lose their temper, and will proceed to try to use physical force to get you in. This is where you stand your ground. Pretend you're a rock. Don't let your emotions come into it; remember, emotions don't belong in training. Instead, be passive. No matter what your human does, do NOT react. The only movement you should allow is turning and walking back to your stall. If you play this well, your human will be perplexed, lead you to your stall, and reassess.

Unless you're extremely lucky it is probable that your human will call in a Trainer to try and 'fix you.' **Trainers are notoriously difficult to work with** but, unless your owner calls in the Hulk or Highlander, *most Trainers can be broken with the same strategy used on your human.* The key is to be a hairy boulder. As I've mentioned before, every time you interact with your human (or a Trainer) **you're either training or untraining** her. Given that, consistency is the key so that your human learns what you want.

If you stick to your guns you will likely never know the horror of sleeping in a flapping plastic nightmare next to weird smelling neighbors.

Best of luck to you.
~Icee

Icee is a 13 year old Swedish Warmblood mare. Her interests include eating, sleeping, and lolling in the pasture. When she's not enjoying her 23 hours a day of 'personal time,' she's working diligently to ensure that her human knows just how woefully inadequate her riding skills are. Icee is a staunch supporter of equine rights and is a proud member of both L.A.M.E.E (League of Assertive Mares for Equine Equality) and S.Q.U.E.A.L. (Society of Queens United for Equine Advancement and Livelihood).

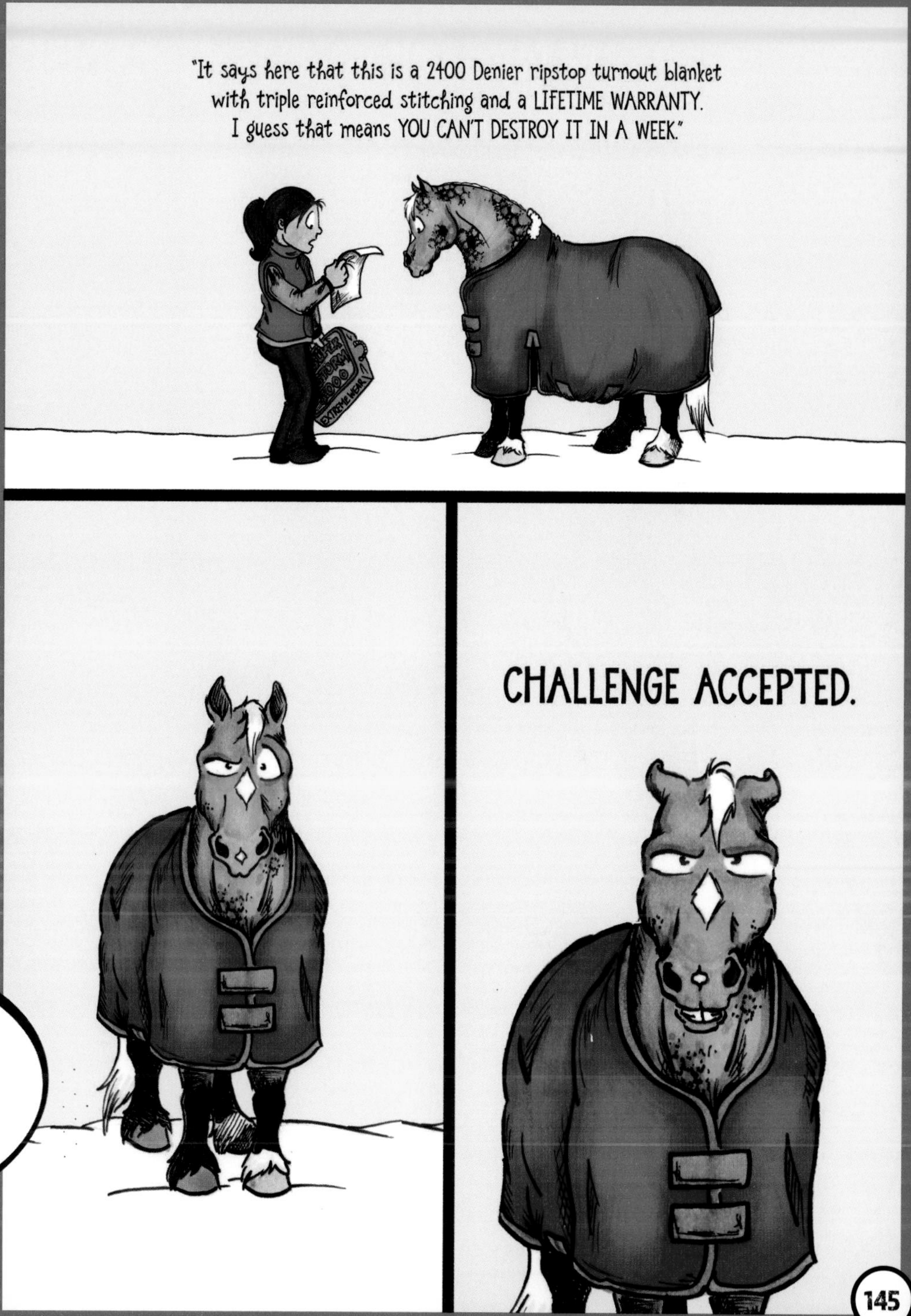
"It says here that this is a 2400 Denier ripstop turnout blanket with triple reinforced stitching and a LIFETIME WARRANTY. I guess that means YOU CAN'T DESTROY IT IN A WEEK."
CHALLENGE ACCEPTED.

Never bait a pony.... Ah, yes, with winter comes the "how-quickly-can-I-destroy-my-blankets-and-make-mom-go-broke" game. It's a seasonal favorite.

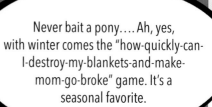

TIME FOR PONY CAMP!

When summer's here (thank the sweet baby Jesus), it's officially time to thrill all the youngest equestrians by tormenting all the most tolerant of equids (and some of the less tolerant too).

"I see you've had a lovely day with the kiddos."

"The next person that touches me is losing a finger."

DAY 1 OF PONY CAMP:

THE RIDERS:	THE PARENTS:	THE TRAINER:	THE PONIES:
"And we get to ride, & clean tack, & do showmanship, & make crafts, & pick up POOP and..."	"Have fun, Honey! Learn ALL the things!"	"You ONLY got me a Venti double espresso this morning?!"	

I'm sure the logic here is suspect at best (much like telling yourself that those white breeches must have shrunk in the closet), but it's at least an attempt to be positive.

These ventures always sound like a good idea at the time.... Because 10+ kids and ponies combined with copious amounts of sugar always makes for a fun time.
I have to admit that, looking back on my riding career, those summer weeks spent at riding camp were some of the best and most influential of my life. I'm eternally grateful to my trainer for sentencing herself to a week (or more) stuck in a bunk house with giggling preteens and their (occasionally) unruly steeds.

MY PONY CAN LIVE ON AIR.

THIS MAKES HIM GIFTED, NOT FAT.

WHEN YOUR PONY THROWS SERIOUS SHADE...

Because you fed *a* cookie to another beast
instead of giving them all to him.

It's awfully shady around here…. I might even catch a chill…. Of all the beasts in my life, Woody (the inspiration for this comic) never fails to remind me of just how important and special he is. A god among beasts, really. And like all pony gods, he's a fairly temperamental little dude. Anyone else have a small tyrant?

When a pony's been put on a strict no-cookie-sugar-anything-actually-palatable diet, he just KNOWS it's utter crap. While he may not know who to blame, he will likely be content to target all of humanity for his cookie-less misery.

Ever feel like the world is just out to get you?

PLEASE DO NOT FEED TREATS!

IT'S ALMOST THAT TIME OF YEAR...

WEDNESDAY:

THURSDAY:

Pony Camp cometh...and all the doom associated with it. Every child's delight and every equine's nightmare.

THE STANDOFF:
When 14-Year-Old Sass meets Chestnut Pony Mare Sass

RIDERS VS. NORMAL SOCIETY

(Adulting Is Hard...and Other Dark Realizations)

It's often been said that one does not simply "own a horse"—horse ownership is a lifestyle. This is the truth. While I'm sure that there are some people out there who only keep Dobbin as a yard ornament (a yard ornament who will, inexplicably, NEVER colic or go lame or even remotely maim himself), most of us immerse ourselves in the equestrian world so deeply that the rest of society can only shake its head and wonder what is wrong with us. This chapter explores some of the awkwardness involved when equestrians happen to wander out into normal, polite society. With our penchant for grocery shopping in tall boots while covered in every manner of gross imaginable, and our pockets full of washed cookie crumbs, we pose a unique experience for the uninitiated. But at the core of it all, even if we look like a hot mess walking in, equestrians are a strong, dedicated, compassionate, fun bunch and there's no others I'd rather call "my people."

Sound familiar? But of course it does.
I'm fairly certain my horses know they own me.
What I'm unsure of is just how totally insane this makes
me. At least I can take solace in the fact that
I'm not alone in Crazy Town.

Sound Familiar?

"I love you so much. I'm going to devote
ALL of my time, money, and
emotional energy to you!"

"I love you too,
Small Biped Predator.

Can I have a cookie?"

Equestrian Work/Life/Barn Balance:
A PIE CHART

☐ WORK
☐ LIFE
☐ BARN

This could be problematic…
or at least explain why so many
horse women are single.

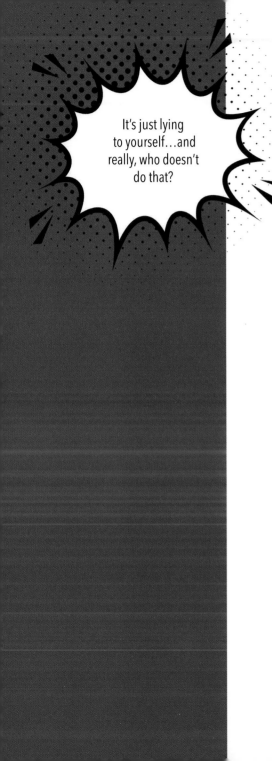

It's just lying to yourself...and really, who doesn't do that?

LIES I TELL MYSELF:
Equestrian Version

1. I'll be back from the barn in an hour.

2. He won't rub his braids out overnight.

3. Buying $300 pants and an $80 sun shirt to wear while wrangling sweaty, snot blowing 1300lb beasts is a completely legit expense.

4. This Lycra hood and sheet will keep my grey horse clean overnight so that I don't have to be up and at the show grounds at O'Dark Thirty to re-bathe him...

5. Wearing white pants and men's formal attire while attempting to show off my horse's athletic prowess makes total sense (even in July!).

6. Buying that 5th horse is a super idea!

7. Caffeine is a staple food group.

8. Baby horses are SO much fun!

9. Whatever that ache or pain is, it's FINE. I don't need to see a doctor.

10. It will be summer forever; there's no such thing as winter...

Spoken Like a True Horseman...

"So, what are you doing friday night?"

"Well, the farrier will be here at 2:30, then the vet and the chiropractor will be out at 4:30 to adjust both Woody and Flirt and also do acupuncture and laser treatments. Then the body work lady is coming to give them a rub down.
If all goes well, they should be done by 8:00 so I have time to poultice and wrap them both."

"Oh. Wow. I didn't know they'd hurt themselves."

"Oh, no, they're fine. It's just maintenance."

"Ah. I see. So have you seen the orthopedic guy about your ankle yet?"

"Naa. That'll be super expensive. Besides, if he confirms that it's broken he'll likely tell me not to ride, which would just be CRAZY."

"Uh, yeah. Of course...."

"Don't worry, I've been keeping it vet wrapped."

"What? It's relaxing."

What? Not riding WOULD, in fact, be crazy. As for spending tons of time and money to pamper your horse, consider it preventive maintenance. Horse people really are a special sort of crazy. I'm still surprised I ever got a boyfriend given this premise. Good thing the boyfriend is really accepting of my fuzzy logic.

"It's just a flesh wound"…and also ego. Always ego. Equestrians are some of the most determined, resourceful, stubborn, tough, strong, stubborn, persistent (and did I say stubborn?) people imaginable. We may skip parties, graduation ceremonies, vacations, and even be late for our own weddings, but come hell or high water, nothing short of death is going to keep us out of the saddle.

"No, really. I'm FINE. I can still ride."

New Tall Boots:
EQUESTRIAN MASOCHISM AT ITS FINEST

"What happened to you? Did you fall off?!"

"No, I'm just breaking in my feet for my new boots."

No pain, no gain? On the bright side, once your feet go numb and you build up enough calluses, it's smooth sailing. So perhaps my hunter friends don't have this problem since incredibly soft, comfortable boots are the trend in *that* discipline. But my fellow DQs have likely experienced the hateful burn of breaking in stiff dressage boots. For some reason, the trend in dressage is for boots to be like stove pipes. If you are waddling like a penguin, they MUST be super-nice boots.

LAUNDRY: A DELICATE SUBJECT

"Did you wash barn clothes and SADDLE PADS in here again?"

"No! Of course NOT..."

I can't be the only one who does this (and subsequently gets in trouble for it). Sadly, all significant others eventually learn to ask better questions, which makes it much harder for me to dance around the issues.

"What are you doing?"

"Getting stuff together to sell on eBay."

"Why?" "I found a new rolled bridle I want."

"Oh….this doesn't look like your stuff…" "GIRLFRIEND! Have you seen my iPad?"

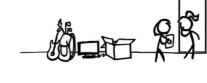

"No."

"I told you that I was her FAVORITE."

"So the barn should go right there & it needs to have at least 10 stalls."

"Why do we need 10 stalls? We only have THREE horses!"

"I know. It's just for extra *storage*...& stuff."

What's a few extra stalls? Of course, I wouldn't FILL them.... When you have horses, there really is no such thing as having "extra" stalls or pens. At least not for me there isn't. It seems that my herd expands to fill whatever I may have available, much to the dismay of most significant others.

My dad made sure my sisters and I had plenty of horses. Subsequently, he never had to look very far to find us most weekends. It occurred to me that I never really did that whole rebellious-teenager-party-until-I-can't-remember-it schtick. I'm not particularly upset by this. It only solidifies my belief that horses are a great way to keep kids (and quasi-adults like myself) out of trouble.

What Most Parents are Worried their Teen is doing on a Friday Night:

How *I Remember* Spending my Friday Nights:

Equestrian Social Skills:

NORMAL SOCIAL FUNCTION:

"We have literally been here FIVE minutes! You can stay and actually TALK to people about things other than horses!"

EQUESTRIAN SOCIAL FUNCTION:

"We have been here for SIX hours! Let's go!"

"But...ponies!"

"Pony, pony, pony, pony, pony, pony, pony, pony, pony, pony, pony, pony, pony, pony, pony, pony..."

Equestrians have "mad" social skills… when they're being social with other equestrians. Otherwise, it's quite possibly a lost cause. I mean it's not that I don't *like* people (okay, so that's probably part of it), I just have a limited amount of energy for dealing with them and would prefer to spend it on those just as [horse] crazy as I am.

Not that I don't get a fair amount of sun being at the barn, but I think it's fair to say I amass an even greater amount of dirt and grunge. Sometimes I'm not really sure which is which.

EQUESTRIAN PROBLEMS:
'Dirt Tans'

"You got a lot of sun today."

"Yeah...I think it's just dirt."

HOW TO RECOGNIZE FELLOW EQUESTRIANS THIS SUMMER...

Equestrian tans...ruining your bathing suit days since the dawn of time. One reason that I douse my arms and face in a gallon or so of sunscreen daily (that and the fact that I'd like to avoid looking like a walnut when I'm 38).

THE IRONY OF HORSE APPAREL:

You're wearing a billion dollars in clothing and gear and you still look like a hobo among the general populace.

Alright, so perhaps this is just me who ends up looking like I rolled around in the muck. Perhaps there are those of you out there who manage to stay sparkling clean while at the barn and then look super chic and fashionable when you venture out into public afterward. *Perhaps.* I'm going to bet I'm not alone in this, though.

When Seen Out and About:

NORMAL PEOPLE:

"Who wears THAT in public?"

EQUESTRIANS:

"MY PEOPLE!"

There's strength in numbers…the horse aroma is also somewhat strong in numbers. You have to love the sideways glances you get at places like Starbucks when you wander in wearing half-chaps and reeking of horse. I did have a girl there once tell me she loved my boots, though. She said they looked "authentic." (The manure adorning them was quite authentic.)

I am pretty sure I own no more than four pairs of shoes and three of those are boots….

EQUESTRIAN HIGH FASHION:

"Have you seen my new Manolos? They're limited edition, just released!"

"These are from the Forge Line. They're ONE OF A KIND - molded especially to fit each foot! They even get readjusted EVERY five weeks!"

BARN CARS...

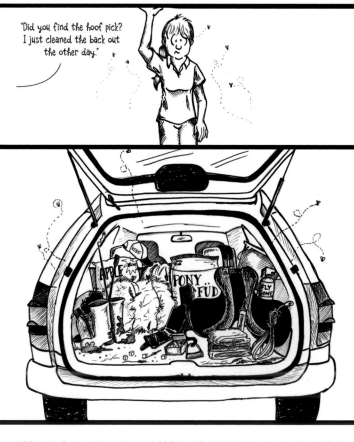

"Did you find the hoof pick? I just cleaned the back out the other day."

APPLE
PONY FÜD
FLY GONE

THE CLOWN CAR'S SLIGHTLY DIRTIER, SMELLIER, HAY ENCRUSTED COUSIN.

You know it's bad when even *you* notice the "aroma".... Only fellow equestrians understand the enigma that is "The Barn Car." At least, I *hope* I'm not alone on this one.

Every time my fellow equestrians and I sit around and discuss just how much time and money we would have if we weren't busy spending it all on horses, we always arrive back at the same conclusion: we would be miserably bored with a life without horses. This either proves that horses are a passion or an addiction (and it seems to me the line between those two is awfully thin).

What I would LIKE to think I would do with ALL my time and money if I didn't have horses...

What I would *ACTUALLY* do...

Shopping for Myself:

"That's cute. You should get it!"

"Yeah…but I shouldn't spend the money. This shirt is fine."

Shopping for my Horse:

"Don't you have FOUR bridles? For ONE horse?"

"Yes, but I don't have a brown one. He needs a brown one too."

Fine leather is ALWAYS a good investment. This just reminds me that I really liked the Schumacher browband I saw at the show last weekend…

Eating a little dirt never hurt anyone…I'm sure eating a little manure is totally cool too. It clearly hasn't killed me yet.

LUNCH AT THE BARN:
Yet another way to horrify your non-horsey friends.

"Hey there! I got us lunch."

"Uh, don't you want to wash your hands or SOMETHING?"

"Na, I think it's sort of like a probiotic."

NUTRITION:

Me:

```
WILSON AM & PM FEED:
GRAIN:
1 Super Vita-Pak
1 Smart Well Gut Guard
1/4 Cup Sunflower Seeds
1 Squirt Extra HA Joint Lube
Electrolytes
1 Scoop Coat Crumbles
HAY: 1 flake Alfalfa and 1 flake Timothy
```

"So, this is his am and pm feeding."

"Ok...it's sort of...complicated?"

"Well, he IS an athlete."

"I guess that makes sense."

Also Me:

"What IS that? Did it come from the show snack bar?"

"Yes. A burrito. Or something claiming to be one."

"Does that even count as EDIBLE?"

"It's FIIIIIIINE."

> Wine is a fruit, yes? It's probably at least a little important. While I am not *quite* this bad with my own nutrition, I am nowhere near as diligent with it as I am with my horses'. What can I say? Carbs are life.

With the Longer Days of Summer...

"Hi, Husband! I'm home from the barn. What do you want for dinner?"

> I honestly think that barns are where time goes to die—especially during the summer when it's warm and light out for hours on end. I always swear I'll be home at a reasonable time, and then *poof,* it's 9:30 and I'm just wandering in.

"Um, you do realize that it's 9:00 pm, right?"

"Yeah! I got done early! Do you want pizza or cereal?"

"What? Toast then?...

I can make soup!..."

Come Significant Risks.

HOW EQUESTRIANS DO SICK DAYS:

"I don't think I'll make it in today. I think I'm coming down with something....Yeah, I'm waiting to go in now, actually....Uh huh. I'm not sure, maybe food poisoning...."

"And next in the ring, number 27...."

"Oh, hey, they're calling me in now. I've gotta go! I'll let you know if I'm feeling better tomorrow."

RING 2

Since horses and showing are basically addictions, I don't think this sort of thing is actually *lying* per se. It's more like creative embellishment.

THE BARN...

7:00 am

"I'm going to the barn for a few.
I'll be right back."

9:00 pm

WHERE TIME GOES TO DIE.

Equestrians are a unique breed. We spend insane amounts of time, money, and energy making sure that 1,000-pound flight animals don't kill themselves, all so we can ride them around and dote on them. If you're not part of the indoctrinated, it seems pretty ludicrous. I get it. And I also get that many of my non-horse friends don't understand what it is we actually do when riding. Nevertheless, the next schmuck who feels the need to tell me riding isn't a sport is getting put on the youngest, rankest beast I can find and sent out for a likely-less-than-eight-second spin.

It's like some sort of time warp. It's a thing, honest. I think there must be a wormhole in every barn–that would explain how I can only be there for a "couple hours" but time jumps forward by something ridiculous...like eight hours. One of you science types should look into this. I am certain MANY husbands and significant others would be thrilled if you could solve it.

WHEN YOU BRING YOUR NON-EQUESTRIAN FRIEND TO THE BARN...
And quickly realize why you don't usually interact with non-equestrians.

Ohhhhh...what she said...?!

"Well, I mean it's not like riding is a REAL sport. You just sit there."

Equestrian House Shopping:
IT'S ALL ABOUT PRIORITIES.

Another reason many horse people are single…because it takes a special someone to recognize the beauty of "Living Quarters Chic." Seriously, though, let's be real, it's way easier to remodel a house than to redesign a poorly laid out barn and ring; obviously, those things should be considered first when choosing a residence.

When you take your equestrian wife shopping for a 'SENSIBLE' car...

What's in your purse?
Certainly nothing like money, if you have horses.
I think we have all been there—that moment when you're fishing around for something in your purse or pocket and suddenly realize you're about to expose just how deep the depths of your equine depravity are. I mean, honestly, how many "normal" people do you know who have multiple pairs of pants with pockets crusted shut from dryer-melted-cookie-sugar goo? I'll give you a hint: none. No one else does that. It's okay, though; we have each other.

Who wants to drive one of those littler roller-skate cars anyhow? I would also argue that having a truck that could likely pull your entire house off its foundation is hugely sensible, since you never know what sort of trailer you may want to haul. Wouldn't want to be caught under-powered.

TOP 10 EQUESTRIAN ITEMS I'VE DREDGED FROM MY PURSE OR POCKET AT AN AWKWARD MOMENT:

10. Hay
9. Cookie crumbs
8. Braiding bands
7. Pulling comb
6. Double-ended snap
5. Baling twine
4. Suspicious empty vials
3. Razor
2. Horse molar
1. Needles and syringes

As it turns out,
husbands are pretty astute.
That or my clever ploys
are perhaps not so clever.

10 Things an Equestrian Would NEVER Say:

1. I don't need any more tack.

2. I can't wait until winter!

3. You know, I'd rather not go browse in the new tack store; I don't need anything right now anyway.

4. It's cool. I'll skip the barn this afternoon so we can go to a social event with your [insert anything non-horse related] friends.

5. You're totally right! Riding ISN'T a sport!

6. My horse doesn't need that new blanket/flymask/boots/saddle pad that's on sale for 50% off.

7. I love it when it's nice and windy outside.

8. I'm just going to resist responding to this random anonymous nincompoop on COTH. I don't need to enlighten them.

9. I hate when my newsfeed is full of nothing but horse pics.

10. Naa, you don't need to buy that second horse.

THE DAY AFTER JUST "LOOKING" AT A HORSE FOR SALE...

"You're home! That's AWESOME; I have dinner ready and just finished the laundry and vacuuming ALL the barn dirt up. And look, I even changed out of barn clothes AND took a shower already!"

"You bought the horse, didn't you?"

"NO! I mean, not technically. I mean I *LIKED* it & all. I might have agreed to babysit it for awhile..."

"Might this be overkill?"   "Nope."

I'm pretty sure I've
never said any of the above.
Particularly Number Two. Number Two
would never happen for me.

ONLY EQUESTRIANS:

"Um, what are you doing?"

"Looking."

"At what? POOP?!"

"Yeah...it's not right. The consistency & color are off. I wonder if he needs more fiber? Or maybe a probiotic. He has a delicate digestive system."

"See? Can't you tell?"

"Are you SERIOUS right now?!"

Shhhh...it happens. You see what I did there? Only equestrians also do double duty as gastroenterologists in their free time. I suppose it could be worse...maybe.

ME: "BEING AN EQUESTRIAN REQUIRES SUPERB BALANCE AND CORE STRENGTH."

ALSO ME: *FALLS OVER WHILE TRYING TO ZIP UP MY TALL BOOTS.*

Equestrians have balance... or at least we'd like to think so. We just aren't always balanced. At least not me. My mother called me "Grace" as a kid, and I can assure you it was pretty ironically. I'm often amazed I manage to stay on top of a horse, given my penchant for tripping over nothing more than air.

MORE LIES EQUESTRIANS TELL THEMSELVES...
BECAUSE DELUDING ONESELF IS AN ONGOING PROCESS.

1. I enjoy smelling like manure, ammonia, and pine.
2. I have plenty of time to finish [insert almost any equestrian chore].
3. Well, I *do* need a new show coat...
4. Horses aren't really *that* expensive.
5. I'm just adding some extra stalls for an emergency.
6. This is the last horse I'm buying.
7. I don't need to lunge him today...
8. That's not going to bruise tomorrow.
9. I'll be back from the barn in an hour.
10. It's FINE, everything is fine. This will end well...

Or perhaps just half-truths. I prefer to think of them as acts of optimism. Seriously, though, I *have* been back from the barn in an hour before... once...I'm sure of it.

Adulting is Hard.

"Put money into my 401(k) OR buy a new blingy browband..."

"I'd just like to point out how dashing I look in sparkles.
Just sayin'."

Ah, adulting...I was lied to about how great this was gonna be. I want my youth back! The struggle is real. I mean, Present Me *really* wants all the many nice and glorious things but doing so sort of puts Future Me in a bind. I wish I could say that I (mostly) did things keeping Future Me in mind....

Come again?
Oh, double entendre....how I love thee.
I'm pretty sure that when non-equestrians overhear certain conversations on riding that my friends and I have had, they are thoroughly disgusted and confused. I am only mildly sorry about this and mostly just amused.

WAIT, WHAT DID YOU SAY?
OR WHY NON-EQUESTRIANS THINK WE ARE ALL INSANELY INAPPROPRIATE.

"Gently now...
Push more; USE YOUR HIPS!
Come, come, come....
YESSS!"

"That's it, there it IS!
That's the spot!
Do you feel it?...
There. RIGHT.THERE. Memorize that feeling."

"Steady. Keep it...square between your legs!
DRIVE, drive, drive!
YESSS!"

"WHAT are you watching?!"

"Um, video from the dressage clinic this weekend?"

RIDING:
Setting the tone for just about everything else.

ME, AFTER A GOOD RIDE:

The world is beautiful.
My horse is beautiful.
A beautiful UNICORN.
Horses are a privilege.

Glitter and rainbows...that's my life.

Come here, let me HUG you.

ME, AFTER A BAD RIDE:

Why do I SUCK? I suck.
I'm taking up bowling.
Don't try to talk me out of it.
Can you just leave now and let me
drink my coffee and stew
in self-hatred?

ME, AFTER NOT RIDING:

*Crashes through the house after
the 47th virtual meeting.*
If I don't go ride RIGHT NOW I may
go on a homicidal rampage.
No, really. The walls are closing in.

I need a horse now!

Horses are such an integral
part of our lives that their inexorable connection to
our moods isn't particularly shocking. A bad ride can cause
a ridiculous amount of rumination, while a good one just
reaffirms that all the crazy, expensive, work-laden things
horses bring are 110 percent worth it. This seems especially
true for those of us who compete, which adds
even more layers to the entire relationship.

"She'll grow out of it," they said…
I guess I just never did. I still go on vacation
and have the overwhelming urge to visit
all horses we may stumble upon. The
uninitiated just shake their heads, but I feel
like most of you probably understand.

The 'Horse Phase:'

Age 2:

It begins.

Age 8:

There's never enough time in the saddle.

Age 16:

What you do on a friday night.

Age 21:

There's NO limit to your dreams.

Age 30:

He has no idea what he's getting into.

Age 50:

What you STILL do on a friday night.

Age 70:

There's never enough time at the barn.

∞

A brief phase indeed.

NEVER SEEN BEFORE

(But All Too Often Experienced)

If you've made it this far into the book, and really, horses in general, you're likely having the dawning realization that entropy is always just around the corner in the equestrian world (if not already staring you in the face). Just because a particular flavor of chaos has not visited you yet, never fear—there's always tomorrow (and the next day, and the next). It's a good thing we equestrians are so adaptable and can laugh at ourselves (mostly).

Whether you've been in horses for 30 years or 30 days....

It takes 30 seconds for a lunging horse to turn it into Amateur Hour.

This is another one of those unfortunate truths... in the blink of an eye, even the most trained of beasts can have you tied in the lunge line and dragged across the ring. I consider myself a competent horse person these days, and yet I don't put it past any of my quadruped charges to take me skijoring against my will.

Oh, I'm sure *he's* renewed. I'm also sure that that means nothing good for me. Why is it that young horses seem to function so well in the arctic tundra while we're frozen in a state of rigid inflexibility?

When you go to ride your young horse on that 20° morning...

"I am RENEWED!"

Although I'm uncertain that horses understand higher-level mathematical concepts, I am convinced that they do understand how the physical realities of those concepts manifest themselves and how to practically apply them (usually to the dismay of their Small Predator counterparts).

Honestly, as gross as snow is, the mud it leaves in its wake may be even more annoying. At least snow doesn't generally devour horse shoes (just my soul).

When your horse realizes the mathematical relationship between the lunge line & whip…

DISTANCE FROM WHIP =
$$r = \frac{c}{2\Pi}$$

* = HA HA HA, CAN'T REACH ME!*

Spring has Sprung.
MUCH LIKE MY HORSE'S SHOES…IN THE GLORIOUS MUD…

Spring...
I'm so glad I sent the blankets to be washed.

TUESDAY

WEDNESDAY

Spring, under the best of circumstances, is mercurial. *Oh, so you thought it was safe to go ahead and clean and store blankets, huh? For shame.* You might consider doing it sometime in June, but best to wait until July if you really want to be safe.

Okay, so maybe the Rubik's Cube isn't *that* easy to solve. But there are certainly far more videos on YouTube that can accurately tell you how to do it than there are ones to help correct the mess of leather that used to be your double bridle. I personally save myself from this nightmare by never taking my double apart. Problem solved.

Solving the Rubik's Cube = Child's Play.

Reassembling your double bridle after you take it apart to deep clean it?

Next to Impossible.

YOUNG HORSE TRAINING:
Adventures in Humility.

"Today, I shall teach you to accept the bridle."

Isn't it funny how often the horses are actually the ones teaching us? Weird. Having brought the Beastlet along from one and a half years, I thought I was pretty knowledgeable. Milona, flaming red, chestnut mare that she is, continues to educate me on how woefully inadequate I am.

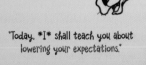

"Today, *I* shall teach you about lowering your expectations."

HORSES CAN BE SUMMED UP SIMPLY AS:

It was all going so well...
Until it wasn't.

Those lightning-fast reflexes, coupled with a total of two brain cells to rub together when something frightening appears, will get you every time. Fortunately, once you've been in this game a while, you get used to the intermittent chaos.

"The farrier will be here today. Could you just HOLD STILL for 45 minutes?!"

"Hmm...what's your best offer, Peasant?"

Young horses...
a new adventure daily.
It would seem that growing
up is so very hard
to do.

"Whoo hoo! Do my new shoes make me GO FASTER?!"

We don't really ask all that much from our horses with regards to their time. You would think they could oblige us by not killing, maiming, or otherwise annoying those we pay handsome sums of money to attend to their every need. You. Would. Think. Sigh.

"How unfortunate. It appears that you remember EVERYTHING from your lesson yesterday. Pity."

I'm sure, just as we once hoped our parents would forget whatever silly task or chore they may have assigned the day before, that our horses are ever hopeful that we fail to retain whatever nonsense that pesky Trainer Lady may have told us during our last lesson. I'm sure, more often than not, we don't disappoint them.

Patchys always do their own stunts...

Ah, the beloved Patchy…
For the uninitiated, the Patchy is a skewbald or piebald horse whose penchant for making poor life choices, and general lack of common sense and self-preservation, makes him an utter nuisance to himself and others (not to mention an annihilative force with regards to personal property). These characteristics make him borderline unrideable by all but the foolhardiest of individuals. *See also: idjit, wanker, spotted moron, and suicidal prat.*

If horses were on social media, I would 100% expect to see something like this. If you've so far been spared this meme, I'll enlighten you by saying it largely features a glut of selfies where people claim to be "feeling cute" but that they "might delete later." I'd condemn it, but then what else is social media for, anyway?

"Feeling cute, might get a stomachache later and try to die."
#FeelingCute #Selfie #IDK

This is not to say that my gelding, Wilson, isn't a treat fiend, but it is to say he's ever so slightly more grateful for whatever my pockets produce than his sister is.

If You Give a Gelding a Cookie:

"MY FAVORITE THING!"

If You Give a Mare a Cookie:

"A COOKIE?! Not satisfactory. DO BETTER!"

Your Horse as a Teenager....

"Oh, hey, glad you're here. So I seem to have come down with hay fever. I'll be needing more hay and some rest.

So let's just not with the hack today, sound cool?"

Although baby horses are terrifying in their relative unpredictability, teenager-stage youngsters (think four-and-a-half to five-year-olds) are truly frightening in their calculated snarkiness. Seriously. The "Frick-You-Fives" are a thing.

I always thought that whole "barn smell" was a sort of perfume?

Life with a Horsewoman:

"Hey, did you get new perfume?"

"Uh....no...I showered?"

"Seriously? Don't you know?
It's the newest in haute couture blankets.
I'm calling it the 'Blan-Kini.'
They'll be all the rage.
If you're nice, I'll let you get in
on the ground floor."

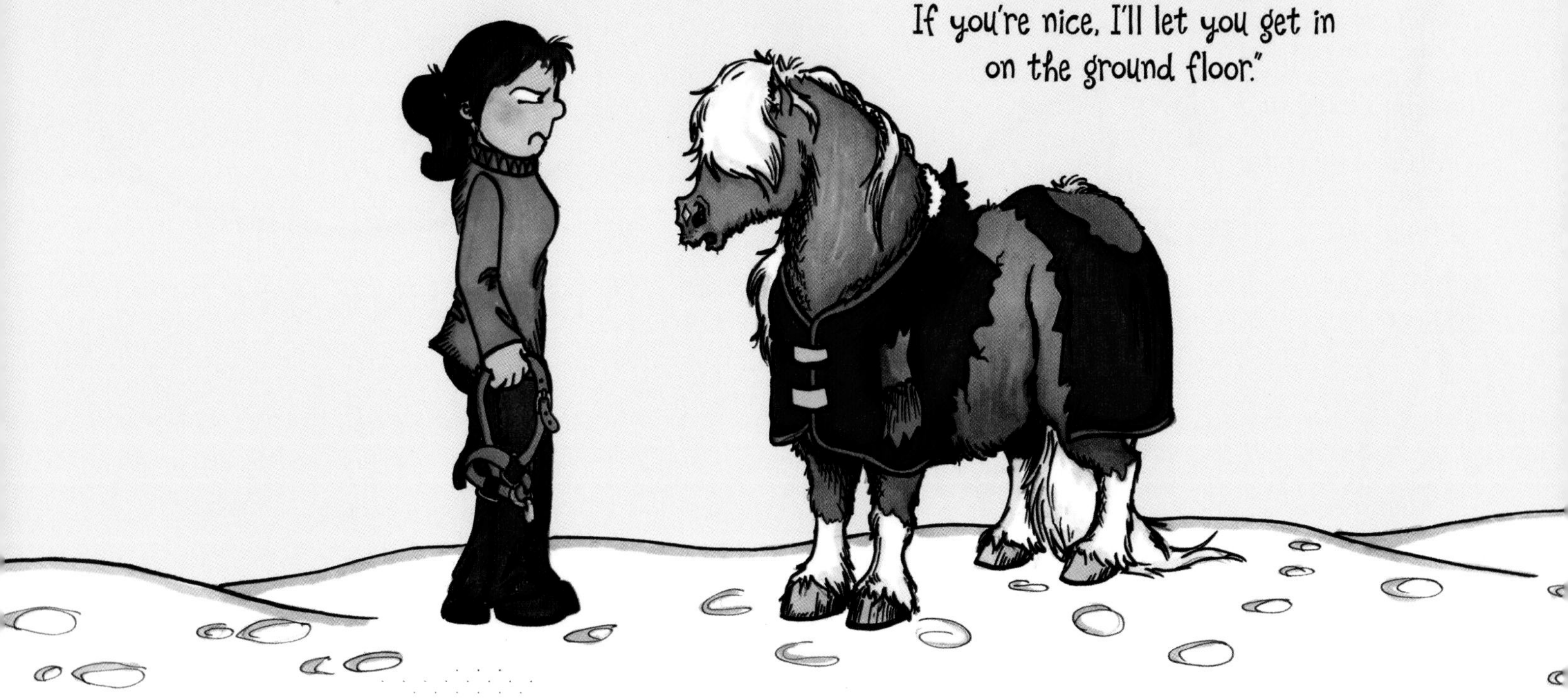

What else is there to say besides the fact that ponies are a destructive force of nature? An expensive, SNARKY, destructive force.

Is there any doubt that ponies see themselves as fierce dinosaurs? I think not. In fact, I think I'd rather handle a feral velociraptor than a small, feral pony.

Horses and the equestrian lifestyle are insanely rewarding...and insanely demanding. As much as we love it, there is no doubt that there are times when a break is necessary. After all, you can only clean so many runs, mow so many pastures, work so many horses, and spend so many hours a day juggling things before your brain cells melt together (or just spontaneously implode).

SOMETIMES,
When you own your own farm & multiple steeds...

Not that I think my vet would be susceptible to such wiles, but I certainly wouldn't put it past any of my shifty wards to proposition her.

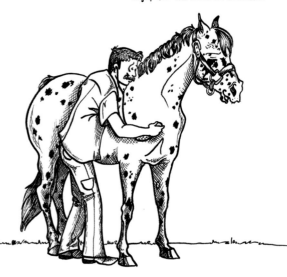

"Pssst, Hey, Doc!
I could make it VERY worth your while to suggest a nice turnout layup for the next six months..."

'SELF-GUIDED' FIELD TRIP:

How your baby dressage horse tells you he has aspirations of being an eventer.

Sometimes, despite their fabulous breeding and our very best intentions, our horses just aren't on the same page with what their future career should be. And of course, other times, baby horses are just snarky idjits. It's really a toss-up.

THE REAL DRESSAGE BARN DRAMA:

"Have you heard? Rumor has it they're sending WeltGit to a COWBOY!"

"A COWBOY?! That's awful. They don't even use sugar cubes!"

It's no secret that I am a hot mess—a dirt-attracting sort of individual. Which means it's no surprise that I am not one of the ladies at the barn who looks like she stepped out of a Goode Rider® ad. Even still, the amount of horse grime and the speed with which I can accumulate it is nothing short of astounding.

And here you all thought the juicy barn drama revolved around Karen hogging the "good" cross-ties and Marge using natural horsemanship to teach her horse to piaffe. In all seriousness, I have often wondered what sort of stories we'd be regaled with if our horses cared to share them.

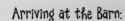

Arriving at the Barn:

Fifteen Minutes Later:

"Hey there! You're not usually at the barn on Monday?"

"Yeah, I took a mental health day."

I mean, I'm not *complaining*, per se. No one WANTS a colic. But I *am* saying that it would be super if my horse could avoid crying wolf (or at least have the decency to look a little punky when the vet does show so I don't look like an overly anxious idiot).

I think we can all concur that this whole adulting thing is totally overrated (for the record, eight-year-old me would definitely not recommend it, despite her initial desire to be a grown-up). But even amidst the chaos that horses can be, I continually find that they do help ground me (even if sometimes it's literally in the arena footing…).

MY HORSE COLICKING:

Me: "I need you NOW; he must be DYING!"

MY HORSE 15 MINUTES LATER WHEN THE VET ARRIVES:

My Horse: "?"

Every Barn has One...

"So, I don't know what plans you had for today but feel free to go ahead and cancel them..."

You know that horse that just can't seem to stay out of harm's way? Yeah, me too. He's usually one of mine. Rest assured he will *never* do anything life-threatening, only expensively career-ending.

Whether you're a dressage rider with ample time to plan and prepare before your test, or a hunter rider perpetually doing the "hurry up and wait" game, this is always the case. There are no exceptions.

HORSE SHOWING:
2 Minutes Until Your Ride? Like Clockwork!

IT.NEVER.FAILS.

Why is this?
It must be one of those
immutable laws of
nature or some
such hooey.

As much as my farrier may like
my horses, I can't say that he *loves* their
shenanigans that result in him needing to
make multiple visits to see them. This
is what wine (or bourbon?) is for—smoothing
that sort of nonsense over.

Quality Time:

"Gee, aren't you enjoying seeing me this week?
For the FOURTH TIME? I know what you're thinking:
don't worry, I LOVE you too."

LEGITIMATE LIFE QUESTIONS:

"But for real?
Why would you have a boyfriend
when you can have a horse?!"

Ponies really are
wee masterminds of absolute
evil doings, all wrapped up in a
fluffy, nearly irresistible package.

While I could perhaps argue
both sides of this little conundrum,
I feel compelled to point out that it's far
easier to sell a horse that doesn't work
out than a husband. Just sayin'.

"Look, Kid.
You just sit there and think you're
in charge while I chart the most
expedient route to deposit you in
the shrubbery."

189

I mean, you *could* make this statement elsewhere, if you wanted to endure the resulting awkward stares and quizzical expressions from all the non-horse people.

How do you go to the grocery store?
YEAH, ME TOO.

FILED UNDER 'THINGS YOU CAN ONLY SAY AT THE BARN':

"He feels bigger than he looks!"

I could pretend that I'm sorry, but that would be a lie. My time-management skills are shoddy enough that they virtually guarantee there's no way I'm going to allocate enough time to get cleaned up and still actually make it to the store before midnight. As a bonus, though, it does keep most respectable people at a safe distance.

The moment that you realize there are
ACTUAL DRAGONS on the cross country course...

As a native Floridian, I can attest to the fact that this is a legitimate possibility. Now whether these sorts of dragons are any more frightening than a high Thoroughbred or Warmblood may be questionable (in many situations, I might well prefer to try my luck with the gator).

Horses are ingenious creatures, particularly when trying to sort out how to get themselves into otherwise inexplicable situations. In my experience over the years, trailering provides them an ideal opportunity for baffling mischief. It's like some sort of Houdini box on wheels.

TRAILERING FUN:

"Be CIVILIZED; it's literally FIVE minutes down the road...."

AS WE KNOW, FIVE MINUTES IS MORE THAN ADEQUATE FOR MASS DESTRUCTION.

#Winning
We've all been on that horse.

Because some horses are surer of their greatness than others—for better or worse. Cheeky buggers.

EXPECTATION vs REALITY:
Training the Young Horse

EXPECTATION: REALITY:

The joys of bringing
along youngsters are never-ending;
I am partial to the ones that
remind me of my own
mortality.

A disgusting labyrinth of sorts.
Honestly, there is never a time I don't regret
using polo wraps: when I put them on, when I take them
off (in a hot, wet, sweaty mess), when I have to rewrap them,
when I rewrap them incorrectly the first time and get to do it all
again, and of course when I have to untangle them
for some ungodly amount of time before enduring
the pain and hassle of dealing with
them once more. Ugh.

UNTANGLING POLO WRAPS FROM THE WASH:

Skill Level: Expert Problem Solver

My Horse's Motto:
There's never a bad time for snacks.

I can't say that I disagree entirely, at least not on principle.

When non-horse people ask me what it's like riding young dressage horses, the best approximation I can give them is that it's the closest thing I can imagine to riding baby dragons. Both are just as likely to be breathing fire, flying through the air, and/or actively trying to dismember you. Of course, I do believe the dragons might be slightly braver.

UPPER LEVEL DRESSAGE PROSPECT:
Not even kidding.

THANKS

As with most things in life, it takes a village (or a small mob) to get things done. This collection of equine shenanigans exists today due to the inspiration and support of so many wonderful people; I would be remiss in failing to acknowledge the contributions of these superb enablers.

At the forefront are my parents, Tony and Robin Schmidt, for not only supporting but *nurturing* my grossly expensive and addictive horse habit, and also for instilling in my sisters and me the ability to find the humor in life's absurdities, the belief that anything is possible, and the knowledge that chasing dreams isn't a foolhardy endeavor. Whether I was drawing Mickey Mouse on the bathroom wall with Mom's lipstick at age three or dragging home a "rescued" Miniature Horse in the back of a Mustang convertible at age sixteen, they never failed to support my insanity and find the humor along the way. They have been my exemplars in life as well as my very best friends, and I am all the better for it.

In addition to my parents, I must thank my sisters, Taylor Childers and Madison Schmidt, who, despite my occasional atrocious behavior as an older sister, have never failed to be my cheerleaders and cohorts. An adolescence spent together, showing in everything from dodgy local shows, to rated USEA shows, to HITS, to reining, and countless hours braiding, mucking, and occasionally being launched into the arena footing by a Craigslist project pony, inspired many of the comics in this book. Even though we occasionally wanted to maim each other—and Madison often would have preferred to be anywhere but at a horse show—there was never a shortage of love or laughter, and I cannot think of a better way to have grown up or anyone I'd rather have in my corner.

Beyond my family, I have been incredibly privileged to have had guidance and support from many wonderful friends within the equestrian community. From trainers who have helped me develop in the sport, to farriers and vets who have kept my beasts going along the way, to the fabulous clients and fellow riders on the often tumultuous, occasionally downright ludicrous, but genuinely fulfilling equestrian journey with me, all have contributed in some way both to the person I am and the art I've produced. I love and appreciate you all.

And finally, a special thanks to my partner in crime and horse show buddy extraordinaire, the other half of Team Neurosis and fellow Baby Dragon Wrangler, Michele Ting. Our horse showing exploits and Warmblood hijinks have inspired a library's worth of books. Certainly, the last decade of horse shows could never have been as hilariously magical without your snark, OCD, and appreciation for pumpkins. You're the best, even with your inexplicable love of snow.

Morgane Schmidt is a native Floridian who recently made the move back to the swamp after a decade's hiatus living in Reno, Nevada, where she has, in fact, confirmed her suspicion that snow is utterly worthless. She started her comic *The Idea of Order* way back in 2011 while bored out of her mind in Clovis, New Mexico. The comic largely focuses on the humorous absurdities within the equestrian world and was inspired by the equestrian favorite "Thelwell" series. *The Idea of Order* was named as an allusion to the Wallace Stevens poem "The Idea of Order at Key West." Given that horses are inherently entropy, despite one's best efforts, the title seemed amusingly fitting. As an English major and self-professed nerd, Morgane often alludes to various literary works and pop culture within her comics.

In her professional life, Morgane works in a marketing capacity for a tech company based in Boulder, Colorado. She also trains a few dressage beasts on the side and occasionally does commissioned artwork.

Although Morgane has run the gamut of equestrian disciplines–including a short stint as an eventer before she admitted to herself that she was a weenie–her favorite is dressage, as it suits her masochistic, marginally OCD, perfectionist tendencies. To date she has completed her USDF bronze and silver medals and is currently working on her gold.

Morgane's life these days is largely ruled by Woody, a 14.2-hand snarky Quarter Horse; Willie, a charmingly cheeky KWPN gelding; Milona DG, a four-year-old-KWPN chestnut mare (you can make your own inferences there); Bowie, a Great Dane with a personality as unwieldy as he is; and Goblin, a tiny terror Frenchton who is entirely convinced he's running the entire Schmidt show. This motley crew and their incessant shenanigans are responsible for many of the comics in this book (and I am sure many more to come).

Woody

Bowie

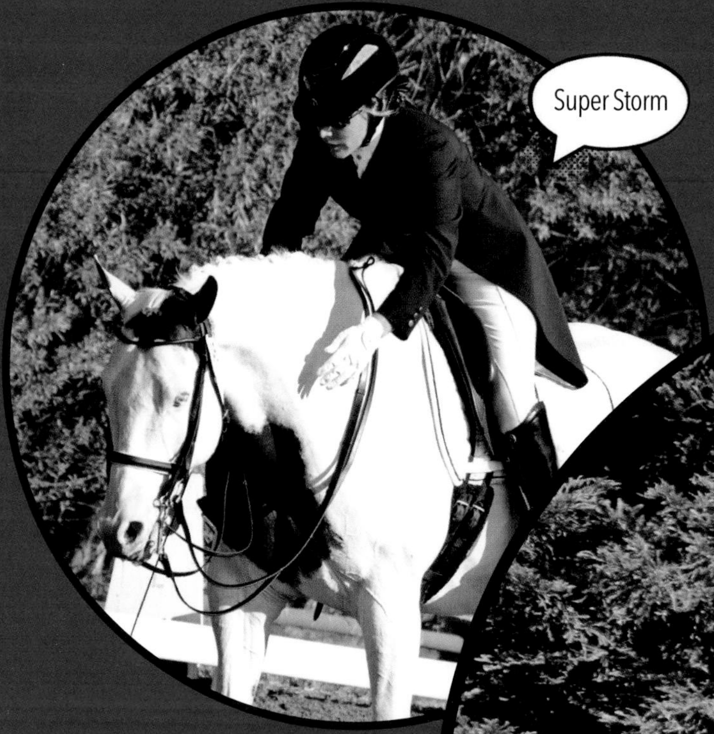
Super Storm

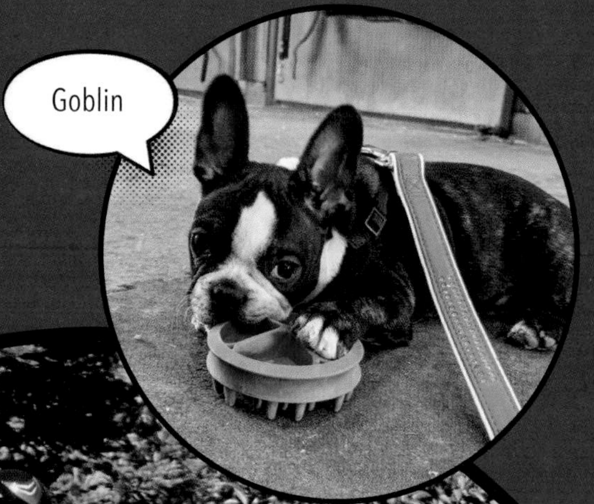
Goblin

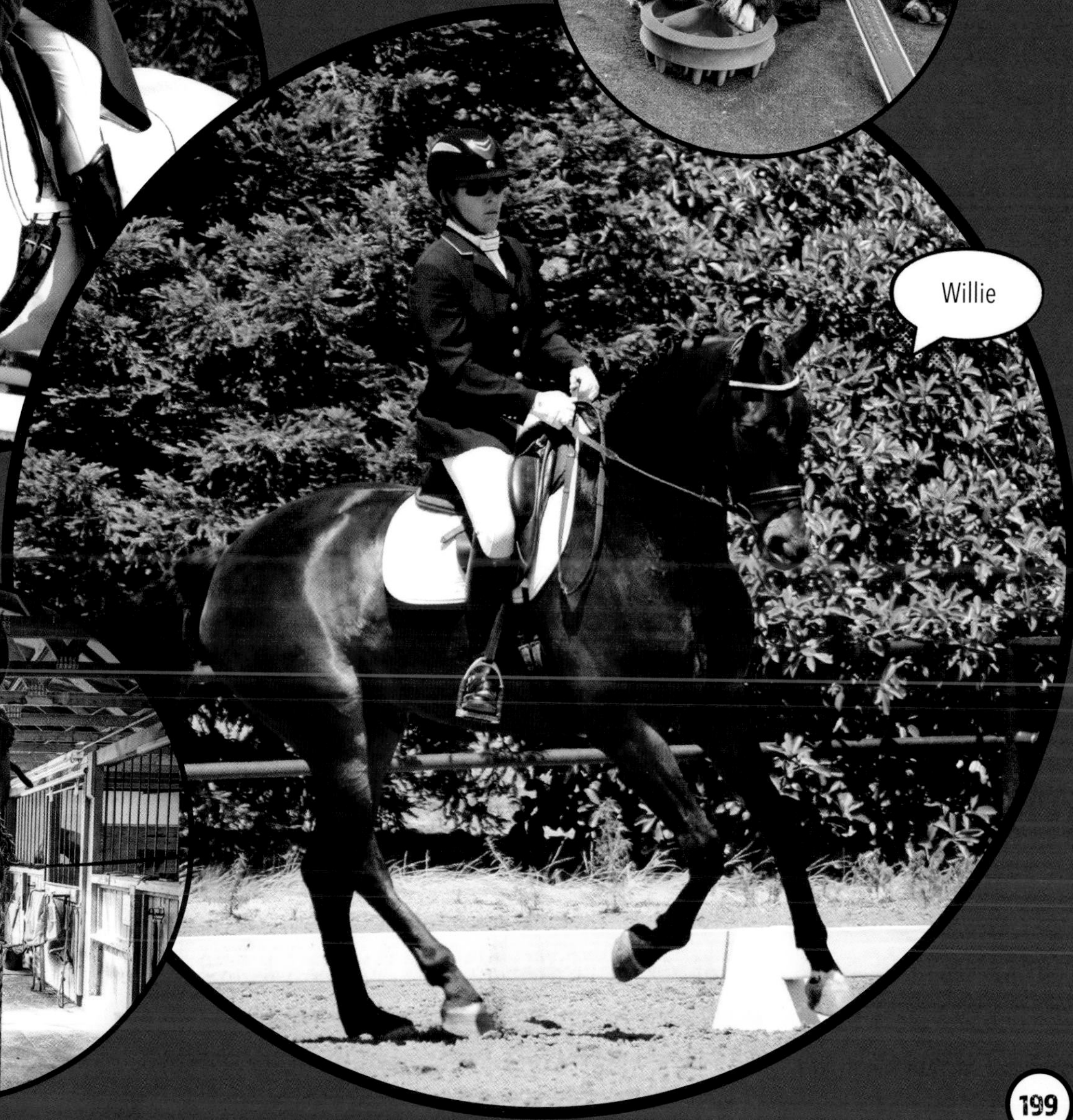
Willie

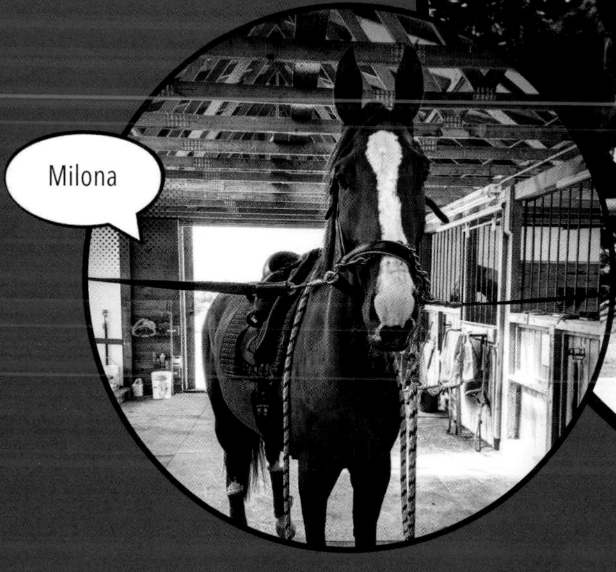
Milona

Follow
The Idea of Order

www.TheIdeaofOrder.com
@the.idea.of.order